NORTH CHESHIRE

Edited by Dave Thomas

First published in Great Britain in 1998 by
POETRY NOW YOUNG WRITERS
1-2 Wainman Road, Woodston,
Peterborough, PE2 7BU
Telephone (01733) 230748

HB ISBN 0 75430 139 7
SB ISBN 0 75430 140 0

FOREWORD

With over 63,000 entries for this year's Cosmic competition, it has proved to be our most demanding editing year to date.

We were, however, helped immensely by the fantastic standard of entries we received, and, on behalf of the Young Writers team, thank you.

The Cosmic series is a tremendous reflection on the writing abilities of 8-11 year old children, and the teachers who have encouraged them must take a great deal of credit.

We hope that you enjoy reading *Cosmic North Cheshire* and that you are impressed with the variety of poems and style with which they are written, giving an insight into the minds of young children and what they think about the world today.

CONTENTS

Daniel Woolfenden	59
James Shelton	60
Jenny Porter	60
Ben Reid	61
Melissa Bates	62
Alastair Bealby	62
Megan Coleshill	63
Alexandra Wild	64
Toni Wood	64
Jane Brown	65
Laura Dooley	66
Emily Reid	66
Catherine Warwick	67
Ben Smith	67
Jacob Pike	68
Michael Bates	68
Amy Coombs	69
Elizabeth Ardolino	69
Claire Bates	70
Sophie Cook	70
Oliver James Robinson	71
Kyle Belt	71
Hannah Louise Firth	72

St Luke's CE Primary School, Warrington

Callum Ashton	72
Daniel Crompton	73
Jon Dutton	73
Emma James	74
Sam Hughes	75
Michael Geeleher	76
Holly Yates	77
Kerri Dawber	78
Helen Litton	79
Catherine Pennington	80
Joshua Felton	81
Caroline Fairhurst	82
Timothy Isherwood	83

Katharine Fox	84
Neil Holland	85

St Matthew's CE Primary School, Warrington

Vicky Lewis	85
Grace Hatton	86
Gareth Rowlands	86
Stuart McArthur	87
Adam Speers	88
Peter Morgan	89
Natalie Gregson	89
Jonathan Henshaw	90
Ashley Platt	90
Natalie Heesom	90
Sophie Mills	91
Jenny Hill	91
Jonathan Nesbitt	91
Nicola Wright	92
Adam Burgess	92
Justin Massey	93
Michael Foat	93
Emma Johnson	94
Robert Cooper	94
Patrick Hughes	95
Harriet Batey	95
Jennifer Milner	96
Elizabeth Evans	96
Victoria Semple	97
Chris Sutcliffe	97
Lauren Massey	98
Stephanie Clements	98
Stephen Platts	99
Chris Nesbitt	99
Emma Perris	100
Jonathan Gee	100
Anna Mathew	101
Kirsten Taylor	101
Sally Pitcher	102

Woolston CE Primary School

THE POEMS

CONKERS

Conkers are shiny brown
Falling to the ground.
Small and big and middle-sized too.
Children in the playground having conker matches,
Conkers being hit.
Soon the conker cracks,
Then it loses its strength,
Then it cracks again.

Then it falls to the ground
Like a dead leaf falling to the ground.
Soon a child stamps on it then the conker loses its shell.
Then its in little pieces scattered all over the ground.

Rebecca Woodward (11)
Alderman Bolton Junior School

IN THE PARK

Sitting on a dirty old bench,
Watching children play,
Over the fence,
Shining brown leaves falling down,
Landing in the big playground.

Spinning on the roundabout,
Getting giddy, hear us shout,
Coming off feeling dizzy,
Playing games, we've been so busy,
Swinging on the swings
We're glad,
But going home makes me sad.

Karl Jones (10)
Alderman Bolton Junior School

THE TINY MOUSE

There was a tiny mouse
Who lived in a haunted house
Every time he heard another mouse squeak
He thought it was a ghostly creak.

Upon an early summer's day
Two little boys came to play
They bounced their balls up and down
That made the mouse pull an angry frown.

Then the winter came again
The mouse was cold and in pain
God bless this little tiny mouse
Who had to put up with this in the haunted house.

Daniel Costello (11)
Alderman Bolton Junior School

AT WESTY PARK

As I was in Westy Park
I saw old ladies walking
Walking their dogs
Mums and babies
Babies crying
It's a lovely day.

Shouting children
Children playing on red monkey bars
On yellow slippery slides
Mums putting babies on red squeaky swings.

I see energetic adults
Running about the place
Sometimes I see skating scallywags
I might see spinning children on the roundabout
I hear a five-year-old on a climbing frame
A shiny blue climbing frame.

Lindsey Arnold (10)
Alderman Bolton Junior School

BONFIRE NIGHT

Bonfire night the stars are bright
Rockets shooting out of sight
Roman candles, Catherine wheels
Can you hear the baby's squeals?

Dogs bark loudly,
People act proudly
Of their lovely fireworks.

You can't get to sleep with bangs
Dogs tear the chairs with their fangs.

You wake up in the morning
You realise it's still dawning,
You're about to go back to sleep
When you've got to sweep the ashes
From your bonfire.

Gary Fogg (11)
Alderman Bolton Junior School

GHOSTS

Kind they may be,
But they're not to me,
They haunt our houses,
Eat our tea,
They pick on my sisters,
Pop my blisters,
They call me names,
They ruin my games . . .
              I hate ghosts!
My friends are always telling me,
There're no such things as ghosts,
I still do not believe them,
There are such things as ghosts,
They're spirits from the dead,
They haunt you in your bed,
I stand upon their graves,
I *must* be very brave!

Nicola Wright (11)
Alderman Bolton Junior School

EXTRAORDINARY

There once was an alien from outer space
Who didn't come from the human race
He came from a planet far away
In the galaxy *Nova Bay.*

He was green with goggle eyes
His favourite food was mince pies
Human earthlings he did scorn
So he blew his silver horn.

So when all his friends had come
A mini war had just begun
They blocked out the sun
With their exploding laser gun.

Some of us died of lack of food
So now I'm in a very bad mood
Now the sunshine's gone away
We won't see another day.

Kelly Lafferty (11)
Alderman Bolton Junior School

WESTY PARK

It's a cold early morning,
I'm off to the big park.
I'm going to have,
All the excitement,
My imagination can take.

Playful pets running,
Running round, round.
The really red roundabout.
Slippy, slidy, silvery slide,
Bouncing boinging,
Beautiful blue balls,
Floating, floating,
Footballs flying freely,
Jumping,
      Jiving,
            Joyfully
                  Away.

Donna Foster (11)
Alderman Bolton Junior School

THE NIGHT BEFORE DAD ARRIVES HOME

Everything's silent.
I'm awake.
Tomorrow's the day dad comes home.
I can't wait.
I think of him,
I think and think.
Then I fall asleep.
I wake up in the morning.
I just can't wait to see him.
Then I look out of the window.
I see dad!
I run downstairs to meet him.
It's early morning.
Everyone's asleep but me and dad.
I sit on dad's knee
I'm happy to be with him again.
He tells me about the war,
And the things he saw.
I really missed you
When you were away
Now you're back with me again.

Aysha Sheikh (9)
Bradshaw Hall Junior School

HUMPTY DUMPTY WENT TO THE MOON

Humpty Dumpty went to the moon,
On a supersonic flying spoon,
The spoon got bent,
Humpty Dumpty said he didn't care.
But for all I know, he's still up there!

Gavin Lau (8)
Bradshaw Hall Junior School

MY JOURNEY TO AND FROM THE PLANETS

On Mars there're,
Big heavy boulders,
Weighing down my shoulders,
There're cracks in the earth,
About as big as the waves when you surf,
It's just too hot,
For our rocket-like cot.

All aboard,
Alfred pull the cord,
And we're off to Pluto.

On Pluto it's freezing cold,
With bumps millions of years old,
Martians live there,
Even though they have no hair,
On Pluto there's no school,
But instead, a diving pool,
Pluto's far too cold for us.

All aboard,
Alfred pull the cord,
And we're off to Saturn.

On Saturn everything's a bore!
There's a horrible floor,
And nothing to do,
You can't even watch cows moo,
The view is flat,
Just like a mat.

All aboard,
Alfred pull the cord,
And home we go,
Back to Earth.

Samantha Walters (9)
Bradshaw Hall Junior School

WITHOUT DADDY (1944)

At night I see the stars shine overhead,
Without daddy, no happiness.
When I arise,
There's not a star left in the skies.

Without daddy and his alarm clock
I'm late for school.
In the morning
Daddy isn't here to put my gas mask on.
It is hard to put on.

After school daddy doesn't pick me up.
It's not fun without daddy.

On a Tuesday after school,
My mum has a really good surprise for me.
She says 'Your dad's back!
He's at home eating something.'
I rush home,
And see daddy at home, safe and sound.
I jump with joy, I say *'Yippee!'*
Today is the happiest day of my life.

Lisa Chen (8)
Bradshaw Hall Junior School

GOING TO THE MOON

What I dream about most is,
Going to the moon,
I don't care how I get there,
On a saucer or a spoon,
What I dream about most is,
Going to the moon.

Maybe I'll meet
Some aliens,
Maybe they only eat prunes,
I really don't mind about that but
What I dream most
About is going to the moon.

Amy Mook (9)
Bradshaw Hall Junior School

SCHOOL ON FIRE

'Quick, quick, out of school!'
'Fire! Fire!' shouts Paul.
'Everybody line up out of school.
Right now - in the playground!
Listen up! I am going to call the register -
Paul, George, John, Adam, Chris.
Wait a minute! Where's Michael?
'I remember, he went to the loo,'
'Quick, quick, in school as fast as you can.
Robert go and get Michael from the toilet.'
'Ok! Michael - quick! Get out - there's a fire!'
'I thought I could smell burning.'
'No time to talk about it - quick out of school.
Somebody get water. Get water!
Hurry up and *get water!*
Well done, John, for getting water.
Now tip it over the fire. OK!
Phew! I am glad the fire's over!
If it wasn't for you, John,
A very good friend of ours was very nearly gone.'

Christopher Walker (9)
Bradshaw Hall Junior School

THE NOISE

It was a wet and windy night
when I woke up in a fright
I thought I heard something
down the stairs, so I put on my
slippers and my dressing gown
Sat on my bed then went down.
Into the living room I did go,
The noise was still there
but very low.
Into the kitchen I did go
I pulled the back door to have a look,
But it was stuck!
I popped my head out of the window
I was very brave, I never cried.
All of a sudden I felt fine,
My mum had forgotten to bring the washing
in off the line.
That was the noise!

Laura Street (9)
Bradshaw Hall Junior School

COMING HOME

My dad is coming home today,
He has been in the second world war,
I can't wait until he comes through the door,
I miss him such a lot, I want him more and more,
When he comes home I will fling my arms around him,
I don't want him to go out to another war.

Claire Walsh (9)
Bradshaw Hall Junior School

SPACE

Yesterday I was out in space,
I had a great time and met an alien with a red face,
Then a rocket zoomed past in such a great flash
And was never seen again 'cause it had a great crash,
The space police went to help,
But 'Sorry,' the man said,
'I don't need help,'
Then I floated up to the moon and soon I heard a weird tune,
The tune was aliens singing loud until the rat came around,
Then I got bored and didn't know what to do,
So I got in my rocket and went straight home.
When I got home my dad asked me, 'Where have you been?
You went to the Queen?'
'No I didn't - I went to space in my rocket,
And yes, I put food in my pocket.'

Robert Boomer (9)
Bradshaw Hall Junior School

AT SCHOOL

At school we do lots of exciting things, like
games, country dancing and drama.
At break time we go outside and we have skipping ropes,
French skipping, and cat's cradle.
We all have fun outside.
Also, we go into assembly in the morning and sing songs.
The work we do is maths, English, geography,
RE, spellings and science.

Leanne Taylor (9)
Bradshaw Hall Junior School

A STORM

A storm comes from the clouds
banging into each other.
A storm is something which blows your hat off.
It would blow children into the air.
It might rain very hard and everything
would be a mess.

A storm would sound horrible and loud.
It would sound like a big grizzly monster
making a mess of his food and like
an audience screaming and crying.

A storm would make me feel wet and sad.
It would smell windy.

That is what a storm is.

Simon Bennett (9)
Bradshaw Hall Junior School

VE DAY

It is a special day today
My dad is coming home.
I am excited
I feel like it is my birthday.
I wonder whether he will come home or not?
I see him!
I run and hug him.
We have a party
My dad is back from the war!

Richard Cotter (9)
Bradshaw Hall Junior School

HOMECOMING

I spring out of bed and get dressed.
He's coming today, I am so excited!
After five years, I have not seen him.
Has he got a beard? I am so excited.
What's the time? Only four o'clock.
What shall I wear?
I will have a sandwich, with half a cheese.
The time has come. He has grown a beard
And a moustache too.
But I love him. He gave me a rusty stone.
I said 'What's it for?'
'To remember the war.'
'Where can it go, where?'
In my room.

Aysha Riaz (9)
Bradshaw Hall Junior School

A ROCKET

I have got a rocket
It's bigger than my mum,
She's scared to go in it with me,
But, it is fun!
I put in my mum's best clothes,
But then she thought 'Oh no!'
She came inside to get them, but
I pressed the red button.
Off we went *brrrmmm!'*

Liam Cain (9)
Bradshaw Hall Junior School

VICTORY IN EUROPE

Happiness is everywhere,
There is no sadness in Europe
No one's quiet - just noisy.
Kids are seeing their dads again.
Laughing, giggling, eating and chattering.
Dancing all night in the dark.
War's over, dads are coming home.
Nobody's lonely.
Nobody's at home.
People are having ice-cream and jelly,
Everybody's glad. The war's over!
People are going to Salford to join the party.
Now it's finished people are rushing home.
Happiness and joy are everywhere now the war's over.

William Cooke (8)
Bradshaw Hall Junior School

DAD'S COMING HOME

Dad's coming home,
To see us again,
I can't wait to see his face,
To play, to smile and have a race.

We'll laugh and giggle,
And have a wriggle,
I can hear him coming in,
I can hear him laugh and sing.

Hello, Dad!
I missed you so much.
We'll have more fun tomorrow.

Charlotte Baker (8)
Bradshaw Hall Junior School

LEGOLAND

Legoland
Here we come,
On the bus,
'Trum, trum, trum,'
Lots of houses for me to see,
Shame it's all too small for me.

Lego spaceships
Flying around,
And making very little sound.
If only I was a Lego man,
I'd live here,
Happily getting a tan.

But I am only a boy
With Lego as my toy
So I will use the bricks
To keep me from playing with sticks!

Robert Walters (10)
Cheadle RC Junior School

CHOCOLATE

C aramel sticky and sweet
H azlenut whirl a nutty treat
O range cream fruity and smooth
C runchie with that honey tinge
O ld Jamaica dark and rich
L ion that makes you roar
A stros that take you into outer space
T wirls that make you whirl
E aster eggs are the best eggs.

Charlotte Harris (8)
Cheadle RC Junior School

MOGGIES

We have four
But I would like more.
A pair of twins
Sooty and Sweep,
It's great to watch them leap.
Tiger Suzy clever and mean
They all make a happy team.
Then there's Jasmine, Jazzy for short
She chases squirrels but they're not caught.
She is playful and funny,
Eats too much so has a fat tummy.
Sardines and chicken and biscuits galore
They eat all these then come back for more.
There's hissing and spitting sometimes to see
It's funny to watch as I have my tea.
A door flap means they come and go
They give lots of love so I am lucky to know
These four moggies,
But can you guess
The cat I like best?
She protects the birds
I think this is great,
So always they will stay
Some of my best mates.

Charlotte York (10)
Cheadle RC Junior School

THIS SCHOOL

This school has brought me luck, good and bad
This school has brought me memories, the happiness I had
The memories I'd love to retrieve
But in September I have to leave.

This school has taught me maths and science
How to spend my weekly allowance
This school has taught me how to draw and paint
Also how to be a good saint.

This school has taught me lots of sports
Including one on the netball court
This school has taught me drama and PE
And how to bandage up a cut knee.

This school has taught me an awful lot
What to do and what not
This school has taught me how to write
How to please and not to fight.

This school has given me friends who are great
And one in particular who's a really good mate
I wish I could have it all back but I can't
I feel like crying but I'll be strong, I shan't.

This school has taught me how to swim and to sew
I'm really sad that I've got to go
No school could ever be as good as this
Especially all the teachers that I'm going to miss.

Louise Kelly (11)
Cheadle RC Junior School

A BORING GEOGRAPHY LESSON

I'll be the greatest explorer, the best of the best
Once I've tackled the challenge of Mount Everest
I must pack a suitcase to prepare myself first
I'll start with clean pants and socks and lots of T-shirts
Must bring some paracetamol in case I catch flu
And I'll have to look stylish and trendy too
So I'd best take my shades but now I must leave
I've a very important task to achieve

I'll sprint up the mountain till I get to half way
Then I'll stop to admire the fresh flowers of May
I might have a chat with an old mountain sheep
'Don't chew my suitcase, it's to last me a week'
I'll get out Monopoly, 'Yes yippee, I've won'
Time to celebrate now with tea and a bun
I must be making haste now, I must be getting on
And up the mountain I shall fly and in a wink I'm gone

I'm really at the top now, 'Yes hooray,' I shout
As I rummage through my suitcase to get my binoculars out
I'm on top of the world just look at the view
Help, I'm frightened of heights, oh what shall I do?
I think I'm falling downwards, I hope it's just a dream
I think I'm falling up now, I think I'm going to scream
I'm rushing very fast now, if only I had wings
I think I've had enough of this Mount Everest thing
And all I can hear is that old mountain sheep
Bleating, 'Hey, Liz Hennessey, are you asleep?'
I wake with a start and all I can see
Is my geography teacher staring at me.

Cathy Wilcock (10)
Cheadle RC Junior School

THE ABC

A   is for apple, something you eat.
B   is for broom, to keep the house neat.
C   is for clothes, on summer days few.
D   is for dumb, by the way, that is you.
E   is for egg, yellow inside.
F   is for fish, through the water they glide.
G   is for garden, with grass that is green.
H   is for Hoover, to keep the house clean.
I   is for idiot, that's you as well.
J   is for jelly, what a beautiful smell.
K   is for kick, that you do in football.
L   is for lazy, no pressure at all.
M   is for master, the one that's in charge.
N   is for naughty, when you push and you barge.
O   is for octopus, when angry squirts ink.
P   is for professor, the one that will think.
Q   is for quiet, now let's have some hush!
R   is for rabbit, that hides in a bush.
S   is for strangle, you've breathed your last.
T   is for torch, that they used in the past.
U   is for underestimate, of people think less.
V   is for veil, a bride wears with her dress.
W   is for weary, when you are ill.
X   is for xcellent, this is so brill.
Y   is for yawn, lessons are boring.
Z   is for *zzzzzzz* now I am snoring.

Andrew Livesey (9)
Cheadle RC Junior School

IF ONE DAY I CAN FLY

If one day I can fly,
I'll fly high above the rooftops,
The earth will look like a tiny ball,
The people like dots,
If one day I can fly.

If one day I can fly,
I'll go soaring high above,
I'll fly high above the trees,
And pass by the birds as I go,
If one day I can fly.

If one day I can fly,
I will swoop and glide in the air,
I'll feel the breeze through my hair,
As I race as fast as I can through the air,
If one day I can fly.

If one day I can fly,
I'll pass by aeroplanes,
Clouds will look like cotton wool,
The sky like an enormous swimming pool,
If one day I can fly.

Gabrielle Loftus (9)
Cheadle RC Junior School

THE FOUR MONTHS

December is Christmas Day
Girls and boys come out to play.
May is the sweetest month of the year
And the word is beautiful to hear.

August is the hottest month of the year
And is the eighth month of the year.
October is the autumn time
Then we're back to Christmastime.

Alice Cooke (9)
Cheadle RC Junior School

KING ROCKET

I sit alone waiting to be lit,
Staring into the sky,
Watching my pals go by,
And there I sit, sit, sit
Waiting to be lit.

He comes with a match,
I feel the heat,
My heart starts to beat
As the fire starts to blaze,
I crackle, snap and explode in a haze.

I am the finest of all,
As the whole world stands at my feet,
Watching me burn and soak up the heat,
Fireworks explode crackle and pop,
I am the king and that won't stop.

What colours I can boast,
Oranges, yellows, browns and reds,
'So there,' I call,
'You can't beat that!'
Once a year is all I ask,
I hope you liked me the most.

Sean Morris (8)
Cheadle RC Junior School

MIDNIGHT SLEIGH MECHANIC

On Christmas Eve in '92
Rudolf Reindeer caught the flu
The not so jolly elves went on strike
All at a quarter to midnight
Then as if to top it all
The sleigh decided it would stall.

Santa cursed and screamed and roared
Then he said a naughty word
His screams were heard for miles around
'Where can a Midnight Sleigh Mechanic be found?'
The nearest towns thought it was a major earthquake
But Santa's screaming reached a man named Jake.

Jake was no hero, a local young lad
Who mended skis in the town of Imgrad
He was no sleigh mechanic, but he'd give it a go
So he set off to Santa through the wind and the snow
Santa was tired and red in the face
And his grotto was a dirty but rather warm place.

Jake fixed the sleigh, it was better than new!
And then he nursed Rudolf back to health too
The elves felt ashamed when they heard about Jake
And went to apologise for their big mistake
Jake was offered any reward
Now he goes on call outs on his new snowboard!

Caroline Page (10)
Cheadle RC Junior School

SUNSHINE HEAVEN

Sunshine heaven is not cold,
It is made of solid gold.
When you walk up the stairs,
Of course there are no bears,
Never forget sunshine heaven,
Even if you're eleven.

Wow what a heaven
I know it even though I'm seven
There is lots of treasure,
I can take by pleasure,
But when I think of sunshine heaven,
I am always in Devon.

There're lots and lots and lots of toys,
And plenty of girls and boys,
To play with me whenever I go,
Away far, far, away,
I am called different names
Peter, Paul, Jack and James.

Emma Ward (9)
Cheadle RC Junior School

WHAT I LIKE

Apple and custard and strawberry pie
Blueberry and apple was my favourite tonight
I never want chocolate I never want sweets
I always want apples and custard to eat
I never eat my breakfast I never eat my tea
I want some apple and custard right in front of me.

Caitlin Leavy (7)
Cheadle RC Junior School

THIS CLOCK

This clock has seen every hour,
Every minute and every second,
It has been set over and over,
Every time the clocks change.

This clock has struck three thirty,
Every afternoon,
Feeling lonely and deserted,
As the children run home.

This clock has ticked all day long,
Even during the night it has ticked on,
Waiting for the children to return,
For them this clock does yearn,

This clock hangs upon the wall,
Waiting for the day in which it shall fall,
And be taken to the dump,
Like a worthless lump,
Of nothing.

Sarah Newton (10)
Cheadle RC Junior School

MY BRUSH

This brush has been my loyal friend since I first got hair.
It saved my life when I had messy hair.
This brush has been used for years upon end.
I was sad when I had to chuck it into the monster bin
Where terrible things happen.

I love you brush!

Tom Gale (11)
Cheadle RC Junior School

FOOD

Breakfast
When I wake up
my stomach is empty
my mum shouts out
there's breakfast a-plenty.

Dinner
When it comes to dinner
I have a surprise
my mum has made me
nuggets and fries.

Tea
It's half past three
where's my mummy
I want to go home
to fill my tummy.

Paolo Granelli (9)
Cheadle RC Junior School

HAPPINESS

Happiness is meeting my teacher
and my friends at school.
Happiness is reading all different stories
from all kinds of authors.
Happiness is fun in the sun!
Happiness is swimming under the waves.
Happiness is climbing mountains.
The world brings happiness to me!

Nikki Triggs (7)
Cheadle RC Junior School

REMEMBER ME

Remember the day you came
Remember the hurricane
Remember you climbed a tree
Remember you hurt your knee
       Just remember me.

Remember Christmas Day
Remember the games we play
Remember you went away
Remember I was sad that day
       Just remember me.

Remember we said goodbye
Remember it made me cry
Remember you gave a sigh
Remember, oh why, oh why
       Just remember me.

Tabatha O'Brien-Butcher
Cheadle RC Junior School

SNAKE

In the rainforest where there's dense vegetation,
A snake lies low in anticipation.
Its blackish-yellow body, waiting all day,
For a defenceless little animal to be its prey.
Its thin fork-like tongue,
All slimy and long - senses something in the air,
It's never wrong, yes something is there
It suddenly strikes! It happens so fast . . .
The little rodent breathes its last . . .

Antony Lavelle (10)
Cheadle RC Junior School

MY DOG

My dog went through pain
My dog was thought of as insane
He's walked down a beach,
Cocked his leg up on a tree,
Ruined a cushion,
and gobbled someone's tea.
He's nearly drowned in the pond,
Up his nose there was a pea,
He's slept on the telly
And swam in the sea.
He's been burnt by a radiator,
He's turned on the TV.
He nearly broke a door down
Just to get to me.
My dog has been good and bad
And he's still the best dog anyone could've had.

Daniel Jameson (11)
Cheadle RC Junior School

THE SEA

The sea to me is the sound of waves
crashing on the beach.
The waves are like brilliant white horses
racing across the sea.
The pebbles being thrown
to and fro on the beach.
Corals with the colours of rainbows.
The gulls' calls whistling in the wind.
The rippling of the water -
that's what the sea is to me.

Andrew Muldoon (9)
Cheadle RC Junior School

A PERFECT DAY

A perfect day.
Getting up early because the sun is shining in a brilliant blue sky.
Running downstairs for my favourite breakfast, Choco Curls and
a croissant
A perfect day.
Back upstairs to read my favourite book
And later, outside to play football with my friends.
It's lunch time - cheese on crackers with grapes and a big slice of
double chocolate gateau!
A perfect day.
Off to Old Trafford to watch United beat Arsenal 3-0!
Home for tea and mum and dad are cooking up a barbecue feast.
'Guess what!' shouts my sister, 'we've won the lottery!'
A really perfect day!

Dominic Kay (8)
Cheadle RC Junior School

MY WORST SUBJECTS

I really don't like art because my pictures always fall apart,
I really don't like history, why?
You'll never know because it's a mystery!

Science is a tricky one that really takes some time
What with solids, liquids and gases, I wish I could resign.

Maths is full of nasty things that need a lot of care
We do this subject every day and some don't think it's fair.

For geography we have to do about places like Niagara Falls
And in the middle of our learning, nature always calls.

Ryan Keher & David Brooks (10)
Cheadle RC Junior School

WINTERTIME

Wintertime is when animals hibernate
Wintertime is when Jack Frost freezes the whole world
Wintertime is when a blanket of snow falls to the ground
Wintertime is when icicles hang on windows
Wintertime is when people get very cold.
Wintertime is when people throw snowballs and build snowmen
Wintertime is when lots of people wear warm clothes
Wintertime is when it gets very dark in the evening
Wintertime is when some animals can't find food
Wintertime is when I stay inside a lot
Wintertime is when the rain splashes
Wintertime is when it rains a lot
Wintertime is when I snuggle up in bed.

Catherine Ruane (7)
Cheadle RC Junior School

THIS TRAINER

This trainer remembers the holidays it's been on,
The endless days of fun in the sun.
This trainer remembers the walks it's been on,
The mud it's trudged through,
The gravel it's kicked.
This trainer remembers the times we've been through
The walks on the beach.
If shoes could talk
This trainer could tell tales of comedy and life.
This trainer, a fine trainer,
Now dead of colour and life!

Jenny Klapper (10)
Cheadle RC Junior School

BIRTHDAY TROUBLE

What would you like for your birthday, my dear?
A jigsaw, a puppet, a toy car or a Sporty Barbie?
No Mum, I want some clothes.

What would you like for your birthday, my sweetie?
A skipping rope, a hoop, a train, or a Gymnast Barbie?
No Mum, I want a CD.

What would you like for your birthday, my little one?
A baby doll, a colouring book, a teddy, or a Baywatch
Barbie?
No Mum, I'd like a TV.

Please Mum, I'm eight!

Stephanie Falzon (8)
Cheadle RC Junior School

WINTERTIME

Winter is the time when snow falls
Winter is the time when we all feel cold
Winter is the time when Jack Frost comes
He freezes the world
Winter is the time when ice spreads over the lakes
Children like to play and watch the snowflakes
Wintertime is fun
Wintertime is nice when the world is covered in a
        snowy blanket.
Winter is the time when animals hibernate
Winter is the time when the wind blows the trees at night
Wintertime is lovely and white.

Lynette Jude (7)
Cheadle RC Junior School

NIGHT

As I lie here on my bed,
On my pillow lies my head.

I see shadows on my wall,
A few tiny, a few tall.

I hear footsteps outside my door
A few seconds pass, then I hear more.

The door goes *'Squeak,'*
The floorboards go *'Creak.'*

How could I have been so dumb,
The person was, of course, my mum!

Helen Marie Collinge (10)
Cheadle RC Junior School

REMEMBRANCE DAY

In the eleventh month,
On the eleventh day,
People all around the world
Cheer up and say,
'The war is over, it's over today!'
But other people weep and say
'My son, he died yesterday.'
So in the eleventh month,
On the eleventh day,
We wear a poppy and we say:
'Today was the day when people said
My son is dead, dead, dead.'

Conor Wilcock (8)
Cheadle RC Junior School

THE BUMBLE BEE CALLED LEE

There was a bumble bee,
Who went by the name of Lee,
One day while doing his rounds,
He found a pound!
He cried, 'Yippee, I'm rich!'
But he got into a fix,
When he returned to the hive,
He was beginning to wish he had found five.
When some bright bee,
Reminded Lee
That bees use honey
Not money!

Victoria Harris (10)
Cheadle RC Junior School

UP IN SPACE

Up in space
Zooming around
Are shooting stars
All scattered around
Space horns
Making weird and
Peculiar noises
Dust and stones
All around Saturn
Stars exploding
The sky's unfolding
The spaceship's landing
Was it a dream or was it not?

Leanne Garbett (10)
Dane Bank Primary School

OTHER WORLD

As I look out of my telescope
What do I see
A great big planet
Looking at me
I turn it around
What do I see
A great big asteroid
Coming at me
I turn around quickly
What do I see
Birds with human heads
Flying past me
I look one more time
And what do I see
A great big shooting star
Shooting at me.

Rachael Wray (10)
Dane Bank Primary School

THE INCREDIBLE WORLD

The birds have human heads
Arches facing different ways
Comets, craters, galaxies, horns
The birds were staring right at me,
And the horns were playing really loudly
But then to my surprise
It all disappeared.

Hannah Street (10)
Dane Bank Primary School

WHAT'S HAPPENED IN SPACE?

It's a very strange poem
About up in space
With real live doves
Which have human heads
Planets, shooting stars
Spinning and curling
In the sky
Wow how great am I really here
There's some weird looking creatures
With human heads
I'm not to sure if I'd like to come again
It's so quiet up here, I'm scared of the dark.
The planets are moving as quick as shooting stars
I'd best be getting home now
It's getting very late.
I went over to my space shuttle
And it wasn't there!
Shall I run?
Shall I hide?
What shall I do?
Then all of a sudden
Something went
Boo!

Danielle Docherty (10)
Dane Bank Primary School

ANOTHER WORLD

Another world is far away
If I land there, I am sure I'll stay
Birds with human faces,
Comets so low they skim your head.

A world waiting to be discovered
Left alone in outer space
Weird people and weird birds
Drifting from one galaxy to another
Not wanted.

Jason Williams (11)
Dane Bank Primary School

UNEARTHLY CORRIDOR

Horns, birds with human heads, arches,
Silence . . .
A crater right in my face.
Stars sparkling like pearls or diamonds
The door closed behind me
The galaxies came closer, closer, closer
I closed my eyes
A shooting star dazzled me
Even though my eyes were closed.
Bang! Everything's gone.

Kate Miller (11)
Dane Bank Primary School

DEEP AND FAR

Far and deep through the galaxy
Space friends are gazing at the stars
Looks like they live as kings
In a stylish palace with spinning planets all around
I wonder what it is like to live out there?

Sarah Maher (9)
Dane Bank Primary School

MAGIC WORLD

Magic is in the air
Spinning stars everywhere
Stars, I love them
Ever so bright
Their light sparkling
Sunshine
I love the sight
I wonder what it's like?
The first step on the Moon,
When I am older
I will visit it soon
Spinning planets
There's a steeple
I look everywhere
But no animals, plants or people!

Lauren Murphy (9)
Dane Bank Primary School

MYSTICAL WORLD

Up in space a star explodes
The shooting star flies up and down
With a space shuttle on the moon
Mysterious temple
Planets all around
Alien chickens with human heads
I wonder was it an eccentric dream.

Zoe Haslam (9)
Dane Bank Primary School

IN A WORLD OF MY OWN

It all started when I got into bed,
Doves were there with human heads,
Saturn with a ring full of rocks,
Craters of the moon, silver-grey colours,
A shooting star dashing by
Just a black hole spinning around
Galaxies were there getting me trapped as in a cage,
Stars staring at me,
Horns blowing, but there's no sound,
Then a comet almost hit me!
I don't like this world of mine
I can't wait to wake up from this.

Rebecca Stevenson (10)
Dane Bank Primary School

SATURN'S RINGS

S   aturn's rings made of dust
A   liens that look like birds
T   he moon that was Saturn's has gone puff
U   pside-down-looking temple, looking from different ways
R   unning, running shooting stars up in space
N   aughty rocks floating up in space
    Looking like they are going to play!

Ashleigh Williams (10)
Dane Bank Primary School

WHERE IS THIS PLACE?

Doves with human heads
Horns hanging from windows
Shooting stars flying nowhere
Rockets landing on the moon
Pick up moon rock
Black holes sucking everything in
Where is this place?
Nobody knows
Spaceships with aliens flying in
Watching the rockets landing on their homes
Where is this place?
Nobody knows.

Francesca Howard (10)
Dane Bank Primary School

DEEP GALAXY

Moon craters galaxy black,
Dark meteors shooting past
Rockets making a racket
Exploring stars
Astronauts on the moon
Floating around with no gravity
Fantastic galaxy stars all around
Could it have been a mysterious dream?

Dean McMullen (9)
Dane Bank Primary School

In A Land

In a land far, far from here,
Craters, shooting stars and comets,
Are all around you.
Alien superheros with human heads,
And space horns which they are blowing.
Saturn and the Milky Way whirling by.
A spaceship darting through the sky.
Massive black holes that are very deep.
Fire flashing furiously by.
Oh! In a land far, far from here
Is where I'd love to be.

Rebecca Kinder (10)
Dane Bank Primary School

Dream World

A dream world way up high,
Stars and comets in the sky,
A picture of planets with a ring,
Strange birds with weird wings,
Weird mountains in the distance behind,
Strange stars that whirl and whine,
A dream world way up high,
Stars and comets in the sky.

Emma Allen (10)
Dane Bank Primary School

CORRIDORS OF SPACE

Weird
Crazy and strange
Appeared from a dream
An unusual galaxy stood before me
Creepy.

Birds
With human heads
At all different angles
With arches all around me
Scary.

Daniel Land (10)
Dane Bank Primary School

UP ABOVE

Up above doves and stars
All the planets, Pluto and Mars.

All strange things up in space
All the questions we ask
How mysterious is that place?

Is it a black hole to a different dimension?
Just close your eyes and use your imagination.

Sarah Garraway (9)
Dane Bank Primary School

STRANGE BUT TRUE

I walked through an arch
And immediately something caught my eye
A bizarre comet flew past the window
And then a whole galaxy stood before me
An unimaginable galaxy
With birds with human's heads
And craters the size of the Empire State Building
And then blank
I was back in the temple.

Andrew Holland (11)
Dane Bank Primary School

THE ARCHED DOOR

An entrancing arch
With fierce birds guarding the exit
Galaxies upon galaxies in front of you
Dashing comets flying through the air
Unbelievable gigantic creatures
You feel as through you are looking in
            different directions simultaneously
Close your eyes
It's all over!

Abigail Kinder (11)
Dane Bank Primary School

BONFIRE NIGHT

I can see a guy being incinerated on the top
Bang goes the banger!
Whoosh goes the rocket!
I can see an old chair with the guy burning on it.
There is another rocket screeching through the air.
Whoosh goes the Catherine wheel.
Bright colours fly through the air.

John Whitlow (9)
Norley CE Controlled Primary School

VICTORIAN TERRACE

I visit this gloomy house,
I hear coughing and sneezing,
I smell squalid slimy scum,
I touch the door to open it,
I see dark corners, many candles try to light the room,
I feel the damp wall, crawling with vermin,
I think I would not like to live here.

Lewis Brookes (11)
Norley CE Controlled Primary School

WINTER POEM

The snow is falling in the morning,
Where the winter cold and frost freezes us.
In the winter there are dark days, short days and gloomy days.
The rain is gentle and seeping through the ground.

Richard Fields (9)
Norley CE Controlled Primary School

Poor

The darkness is damp and cold.
I hear the echoing wails of ill children.
The smell is dreadful, as if people had died before me.
I see many horrible things that would make people shiver.
I can taste the poor meal they had a week ago.
I feel scared of what I will see round the next corner.
I can't even imagine who would live there.

Naomi Jones (10)
Norley CE Controlled Primary School

Candle Burning

Beautiful, glowing, silent candle
With a dancing flame.
Overflowing stream of wax.
A volcano overflowing.
Such a little flame can do so much damage.

Mark Williamson (10)
Norley CE Controlled Primary School

Burning Candle

Distracting, hypnotising, like a dream.
Christmas feeling.
Old street lamp on a quiet snowy night.
Greeny, yellowy, melted wax,
Flowing down the side.

Jonathon Hocker (9)
Norley CE Controlled Primary School

WINTER

Outside the window
It's bucketing down with rain.
I step outside,
I shiver like a block of ice.
It's still dark and miserable
By the end of the day.
I'm soaking wet and cold,
I step inside to a warm fire
With my toes like ice-cubes.
I look outside the window again
The rain has turned to snow.
Children rush out and build
Snowmen,
The smell of roast chicken
Coming out of one window and
Into the next . . .
I walk up the stairs and climb into my bed
With a warm hot water bottle.

Charlotte Rigby (10)
Norley CE Controlled Primary School

MY RAINFOREST EXPERIENCES

The rainforest is very hot and sticky
The animals howl and shriek
It's never quiet in the rainforest
There is hardly any light or cold
The leaves are really big and bold
The vegetation is particularly dense and thick
The fish swim round and round
The insects are incredibly delicious.

Caroline Shrubb (10)
Norley CE Controlled Primary School

BIRDS OF PREY

Sitting in the hall,
Children a quiver with excitement,
Three sets of beady eyes look at us
Orange and black.
There's a noise behind the piano,
A message left on the floor
What will the caretaker say?
Out go the lights,
Curtains are drawn
We tuck up small.
Swooping almost silently
The barn owl flies over our heads
Back to its owners out-stretched arm.
Out to the playground with the falcon we go
He glides through the air
Landing on a telegraph pole
Back he headed for his treat.

Holly Somers (10)
Norley CE Controlled Primary School

CANDLE BURNING

Candle burning slowly and silently.
Dancing flame in the wax.
A big volcano erupting.
A flowing stream of wax.
The wick was white but now it is black.
The purple wax is burning.
Wax trickling down the side.
Lots of light from the flame,
But then it is gone.

Paul Baker (10)
Norley CE Controlled Primary School

WINTER POEM

I was sleeping one night while the sky was weeping.
I felt glum
The sky was gloomy, the window was very cold.
The wind was howling loud.
My dog was barking.
Our garden pond was ice.
I went downstairs to let the dog in.
It was so cold the wind whistled against my ears.
My coat was dripping wet it had just gone 8.00
But it was still dark.
The wind was blowing branches off the little apple
                                    tree in the corner.
The grass was soggy and very muddy.
When I went back in I hung my coat up
It was soaking, it dripped all over the floor.

William Davidson (8)
Norley CE Controlled Primary School

WINTER

Any way I choose to go
I can't escape the falling snow
It covers my eyes
Where I walk, it takes my place
In the morning when I awake
It's a dull day,
Rain drenching our coats
Drips and drops falling off my coat
Drip, drop, drip, drop
Weeping rain, fighting the sun.

Georgie Sutcliffe (9)
Norley CE Controlled Primary School

THE VISIT

The door was open so I just walked in
It was very scary
The first thing I heard was a baby wailing
I walked further in.
I felt a shiver down my spine
Suddenly a wild cat jumped up and
Scratched me
I felt a trickle down my stomach
I was bleeding
Just then a woman walked into the kitchen
She had a rash on her face
She put a bandage on my wound
It was dirty
She offered me a glass of water
I refused for her water was dirty.

Samantha Howman (11)
Norley CE Controlled Primary School

IN THE GRIP OF WINTER

In the grip of winter
Days go darker
Nights go longer
Rain buckets down
From the dark gloomy sky
Ice hits the earth
And makes it slippery
So wrap yourself up
And keep warm and
You will see spring be born.

Luke Harding (9)
Norley CE Controlled Primary School

WINTER

Winter is dull and cold.
You pull your scarf around your neck with
horrid wind beating at your nose.
Your nose goes red while your feet go blue.
Children covered in snow making snowballs for
the throw.
With a little clue that Santa's on his way.
Cars won't start, the engine freezing.
Slippery roads and ponds with ice a-covering.
Footy matches called off because the pitch is
water-logged.
This is what I think is different about winter
than any other season.

Mark Eisner (9)
Norley CE Controlled Primary School

WINTER

That morning I looked out of the window
I saw snow, it wasn't a dull morning.
I got changed and I was out in a flash.
The snow hit my eyes.
I blinked, I twinked.
But no snow stopped
The expressions.
I can't explain, I loved it.
But suddenly, it went dark.
It looked as if black coal was scattered in the sky
That was one good day ended.

Helena Jones (8)
Norley CE Controlled Primary School

I'M LUCKY, I AM

Wandering through dark tunnels as mice crawl at my feet,
Filling up with fear as I draw nearer to the terrace,
Knocking at the door, my hand shivering with fear
As I wonder if I should turn back to the comfort of my home.
As the door creaks open a solemn face looks at me.
I step inside and look in horror at a damp dark room.
Mice hang from the ceiling,
Mouldy drinks spilt on the floor,
The smell of sewers fills up the room.
I return to my house,
My fear left behind.
I think how lucky I must be
To live in a palace.

Kerry-Lee May (11)
Norley CE Controlled Primary School

BIRDS OF PREY

Children sitting anxiously and excited,
Birds of prey perched on perches
Brown, pale yellow feet, black beams,
Orange mysterious eyes.
Children laughing at a funny European eagle owl,
A barn owl swooping through the air.
Hawk landing on a branch of a tree,
The hawk's taking off again heading for a telegraph pole.
The hawk's being attacked by some jet-black crows.
The hawk tries to defend himself,
In the end he comes back for his reward.

James Carruthers (10)
Norley CE Controlled Primary School

HENRY VIII'S WIVES

It wasn't good,
To be Henry's wife.
It gave a new meaning,
To, 'Get a life.'

Catherine of Spain,
Was the first of many.
Henry wanted a son,
And she didn't have any.

Second up,
Was Anne Boleyn.
When her head was chopped off,
It fell in the bin.

Jane Seymour was next,
She made his day.
Gave him a son,
But died anyway.

Next one along,
Was another Anne.
When she turned up for real,
She looked like a man.

Next up for the chop,
Was Catherine Howard.
When the axe went down,
She wasn't a coward.

Last but not least,
Was Catherine Parr.
She survived Henry,
Ha, ha, ha.

Liam Flanagan (11)
Norris Bank Primary School

FAST MONKEY

Monkey swings through the trees
swinging from branch to branch.
He snaps twigs and leaves off
while he goes.

The monkey kicks the elephant and teases him.
The elephant runs after him.
Monkey goes through a passage that's very narrow
now elephant can't catch him.

The monkey runs fast
in case elephant
finds another way past.
At last he decides to stop.

The monkey sits down under a tree to rest
but suddenly elephant comes back.
Monkey jumps into a tree
and hides from him.

Monkey lays down under a tree.
Elephant spotted him.
Up he crept, monkey didn't hear him.
Monkey woke up, elephant kicked him.

Monkey lays down
and goes to sleep.
Even though his leg hurt
he was fine.

Rachel Beaman (9)
Norris Bank Primary School

MY BEST FRIENDS

I had a best friend
her name was Jane.
After two weeks
she called me a pain.

I had a best friend
her name was Kate.
She hates me now
'cause I broke her plate.

I had a best friend
her name was Jill.
She's so angry with me
she's ready to kill.

I had a best friend
her name was Meg.
I tripped her up
and broke her leg.

I had a best friend
her name was Nicky.
She was always
taking the mickey.

When they come near me
they make me cry.
They all hate me
I don't know why.

Jenny Sharpe (10)
Norris Bank Primary School

THE CROCODILE GARDEN

I strolled across the path one night.
I heard a snap and got a fright.
I looked around my shoulders.
I saw a pinky thing.
It was a snappy snappy pair of teeth.
I picked them up.
They felt slimy and I thought they belonged to
my grandma up in space.
I imagined that I was being watched.
With eyes all around me.
I was right.
Because suddenly my eyes turned blurry.
And all I could see was green.
Our garden turned into a jungle.
And our pond turned into a lake.
The grass turned into a desert ground.
And all I could see was crocodiles in front
of my face.
I got scared, I got scared out of my wits.
I just wanted to be under the covers
of my bed.
The crocodiles snapped at me.
They glared and stared and I blinked.
I wanted to say it was all a dream.
But when the crocodile came towards me,
I screamed and screamed.

Demah S Al-Gheithy (10)
Norris Bank Primary School

CAT

Knocking over dustbins
looking in for food
getting chased by dogs
when they're in a mood.
In and out of cars
dashing down the street
the only trouble starts
when dogs look there for meat.

Chasing mice down alleyways
snapping at their tails
eating them for dinner
with sauce and roasted snails.
Looking in the pond
for some fishy food
the only trouble starts
when humans are in a mood.

Sleeping under cars
playing with the kids
eating food from tins
then licking all the lids.
Going back to sleep
in the alleyway
now he'll wait
till another day.

Nathan Marks (9)
Norris Bank Primary School

ANT POEM

It moves like us but on six legs
one after another and then the other legs come
it walks over leaves in the grass
over stones and through the mud
and underground and in the trees.

It carries food day and night
then it makes a gang
to carry big food
like flies, caterpillars and dead beetles
apart from the fly - that only takes one
and they eat all night.

It lives in a garden underground
it lives in paths
it lives in soil
in a big brick
it lives in wood
everywhere you look.

It eats almost anything
ladybird skin
leaves
litter
it's an ant
around the garden.

Jonathan Price (9)
Norris Bank Primary School

TURTLE'S JOURNEY

The baby turtles have hatched from their eggs,
They wobble about on their little legs,
The mother turtle has to leave,
The babies struggle to the sand to breathe,
They have to struggle to the sea,
That is where they need to be.

Along that stony sand they plod,
Their eyes half-closed, heads nod,
But watch!
There's a lizard there, with a glittering eye,
It snatches one up as it slowly plods by.
But the rest struggle on frantically,
To the sea, to the sea, where they need to be.

The lizard comes and strikes again,
Gobbles up eight, nine, no ten,
But the mother turtle laid many eggs,
Some still struggle in the dark on those little legs,
Those that are left reach the sea,
That is where they're glad to be.

They have reached the sea, sea, sea!
They are really free, free, free!
Soon some will lay their own eggs,
With babies who wobble about on little green legs.

Clare Longden (9)
Norris Bank Primary School

AFRAID OF THE DARK

If you're afraid of the dark,
Never come out at night!
One other thing,
Never turn out your light!

When at last you go to bed,
Put your light on for the night.
Keep the shadows locked away,
So everything will be all right.

Andy Baines (10)
Norris Bank Primary School

SMELLY POTIONS

Boil the pot till it gets hot
Add a bit of human spit
Add some newts' eyes and 3 fireflies
Stir it well
Till it starts to swell
Now
Add a burr of rabbit's fur
Add some wood soaked in blood
Smoke should rise
So add more flies
Add some rats and dung from bats
Add some hair and a tooth of a bear
Add a skull and a horn of a bull
Add a bolt from Frankenstein
And some coal from the abandoned mine
Now
There should be a lot of heat
Now add one pound of meat and smelly feet
Now the pot has boiled for hours
Now I'll serve it to my friends
I'll just throw in some odds and ends
I'll pour it into a glass
And serve it to the rest of the class.
Do you think they will like it?

Richard Barber (10)
Norris Bank Primary School

THINGS THAT GO BUMP IN THE NIGHT

I am in bed
My goosebumps read
My goodnights said
Darkness has fallen
Shadows are calling

It's ghosts and ghouls
It's werewolves howling
There're bumps and creaks
There're vampires prowling

The moon is full
The bats are screeching
The skeletons eating
The bones of the dead

It's scary, it's frightening
The monsters are biting
Oh no . . . Oh no . . .
> *Ahhh!*

I am in bed
My goosebumps read
My goodnights said
Oh dear! Is it all in my head?

Sean Higgins (10)
Norris Bank Primary School

THE SEA HORSE

The waves rushing past her body,
The cool breeze in her face.

Her blue tail splashing,
Through the big blue sea.

Merina loves to swim with the sea horse,
Riding through the wind.

Trails leaving behind the boat,
It's blue paint matches the sea,
and Merina's back.

Scarlett Bodnar (9)
Norris Bank Primary School

THE FOUR ANIMALS

The dog, the cat, the guinea pig and bat,
They all have an amazing habitat.
They do go away, but they do come back,
The dog, the cat, the guinea pig and bat.

They do go to sleep, they don't cry or weep,
The dog, cat, and guinea pig are very sleek.
But bats hang upside down in caves or trees,
When guinea pigs want their food, they really squeak!

The dog, the cat, the guinea pig and bat,
They all have an amazing habitat.
They do go away, and they do come back,
The dog, the cat, the guinea pig and bat.

They all are just a little bit fat,
The dog, cat and guinea pig, even the bat.
It likes the food, does the cat,
And the dog, on his head, he gets a pat.

The dog, the cat, the guinea pig and bat,
They all have an amazing habitat.
They do go away, but they do come back,
The dog, the cat, the guinea pig and bat.

Daniel Woolfenden (9)
Norris Bank Primary School

I Want

I want a parrot that says my name
I want a hamster that plays a game
I want a dog I want a cat
I really want that jazzy hat
       I want, I want, I want

I want a nice stunt bike
I want a house that I really like
I want some stunt pegs
I really want to try frogs' legs
       I want, I want, I want

I want a fountain I want to climb a mountain
I want it to pour down with rain
I want a pen I want a hen
I want to have my own den
       I want, I want, I want

I want a very big teddy bear
I want someone to cut my hair
I want something that is really tall
I want something that is really small
       I want everything!

James Shelton (10)
Norris Bank Primary School

I Wish

I wish I lived up on a farm
I wish I had a magic charm
I wish I didn't have an ugly face
I wish I lived up high in space.

I wish I got my own way all the time
I wish that puppy in the shop was mine.

I wish I had a mountain bike
I wish I didn't live near Jennifer Pike
I wish I could stay up late,
I just wish I could be eight.

Jenny Porter (10)
Norris Bank Primary School

THE ALIENS THAT CAME TO MY DOOR

I woke up one night and heard some noise,
At first I thought it was just teenage boys,
I looked out my window to see something like,
A spaceship called 'Little Tyke'.
The light beams came down and dazzled my eyes,
When aliens came to my door,
The first alien out had clearly eaten all the pies,
When aliens came to my door.
The next one out looked like some old bloke,
But he even looked like he could choke,
When aliens came to my door.
The ET out was clearly female,
But she was busy writing e-mails,
When aliens came to my door.
Although there must have been thousands,
Only a couple came to my house and,
Since then I've wondered why I found it so,
Boring,
Sitting there all night,
Hiding my fright,
From the aliens that came to my door.

Ben Reid (10)
Norris Bank Primary School

SPLISH SPLOSH!

It's not fair,
The rain's spoiled my day,
I'm supposed to be going,
To the park today.
Splish splosh!

I can't do my homework,
The noise is too loud,
Bouncing off the roof,
Hitting the ground.
Splish splosh!

'Come on' shouts my mother,
'The rain has now stopped,
Put on your wellies,
And we'll go to the shops.'
I splashed in the puddles,
And danced all the way,
Glad to be out,
On this wet windy day.
Splish splosh!

Melissa Bates (11)
Norris Bank Primary School

MUSICAL MAYHEM!

Mum listens to Mumbo Jumbo
Dad listens to Indie
My sister listens to nursery rhymes
While playing with her Sindy

Clarence listens to classical
Veronica listens to Verve
Granny listens to jazzy music
Which makes her bum swerve

Auntie listens to African music
Uncle's music's insane
But the wonderful music I listen to
I play again and again, and again.

Alastair Bealby (9)
Norris Bank Primary School

LIGHT

There's nothing I like more,
than walking home in the twilight
when the sun has finally gone to bed
and the moon
is just raising her sleepy head.
When streetlights are beginning to glow
and the lights in the houses
start to throw their welcoming light at my feet
it's such a shame
that I can't feel their heat.
What would we do
I often think, if
someone
somewhere
had never invented this
wonderful thing
that lets us see when there's no daylight
and makes our houses warm and bright
this wonderful thing is simply called
Light!

Megan Coleshill (9)
Norris Bank Primary School

BABIES!

Babies scream and shout and wriggle
they never stay still at all.
All they do is moan moan moan
and drive us up the wall.

My dad says they're a pain in the neck,
my mum agrees with him.
But then again who wouldn't?
Someone with no brain I think!

Grandma came for dinner
once we put the baby to bed.
She started crying after about five minutes.
'I bet you never get any peace around here' she said.
She went outside to get some peace
and the baby fell straight to sleep!

Alexandra Wild (10)
Norris Bank Primary School

FOLLOW ME

Up the road,
And down the lane,
Through the meadow,
In the rain.

To the town,
And then the farm,
But please don't come to any harm.
The cat will stray too far away,
So child don't follow him today.

Up the road,
And down the lane,
Through the meadow,
In the rain.

To the town,
And then the farm,
But please don't come to any harm.
The cat will stray too far away,
So follow him another day.

Toni Wood (11)
Norris Bank Primary School

WHEN I WAS SMALL

When I was small,
My mother tells me
I used to shout and scream and bawl,
And sit in my playpen all day long
Then sing a little gurgling song.
I also used to wear a nappy
Which didn't make me very happy
Because it was really smelly,
Rather like my dad's old wellie.
I looked at my mum,
'Me that horrid little child?
You must be wrong.'
But she just smiled.

Jane Brown (10)
Norris Bank Primary School

MY BABY SISTER

My baby sister is such a pain.
She burps and cries a lot
but always wets her nappy and chews her toys.
We give her milk to make her shut-up,
but it never works with my baby sister.
As soon as my mum puts her to bed
everything is quiet and calm,
then she's off again
Wa wa waaa!
In the morning it's 5.00am,
she wakes me up by
Wa wa waaa!
Then all day long she sits on my knee.
Then, she just has to watch
her favourites programme on TV.
It's Teletubbies.
Then she starts singing Teletubbies,
maybe not all day long
but she still drives me up the wall.

Laura Dooley (9)
Norris Bank Primary School

AUTUMN

Autumn leaves go dancing
twirling floating swirling
gently to the ground.
They are crispy crackly
crunchy scrunchy.
Squirrels come out to hibernate.
In the woods conkers fall down.

Emily Reid (7)
Norris Bank Primary School

SPLISH SPLASH

Splish splash its tail goes whack
Diving in and out
Making a big splash.
It's a brilliant blue
A long bottle-shaped nose.
That's right, it's a dolphin.
Skimming the waves
Like a pebble
Sleek and smooth.
It's fun to play with,
Her name's Merina.
She looks beautiful
Sitting on the waves
With her friends.
Dancing and playing
It looks so much fun!
I wish I was a dolphin
Playing until the sun sets.

Catherine Warwick (9)
Norris Bank Primary School

A POEM ABOUT MY DOG TRIXIE

My dog Trixie is golden brown,
With black zigzags and a very cute frown.
Dark brown, puppy-sad eyes
A long black snout and very tiny thighs
A dark, black wet nose
Pointed ears and a curl in her tail
And a very sad wail.
I love my dog Trixie.

Ben Smith (10)
Norris Bank Primary School

STEVIE SPIDER

Little Stevie spider in the garden,
I pick him up and play with him.
In his web he catches them,
Flies and beetles that are dead.

He walks on his eight little legs,
Which are smaller than our plastic pegs.
They feel so nice,
Patting on your arm.

Some spiders are big,
Some are small.
Some are hairy,
And some are bald.

Stevie is small,
And has no hair.
I like them like that,
Nice and bare.

Jacob Pike (9)
Norris Bank Primary School

THE KITES

The kites fly in the air.
They dance in the air.
Twirling whirling in the air.
People hold the kites enjoying themselves.
Running everywhere.
Their kites go to and fro.
Each kite is different.
I like kites because they twirl in the air.

Michael Bates (7)
Norris Bank Primary School

THE BABY SEAL FLIPPER

The baby seal,
all furry,
all white,
yet nobody's meal.
The baby seal is called Flipper,
and is a bit of a nipper!
Flipper flaps his flippers
When he wants his tea.
Crashing along the ice
'I'm going to get my tea' he hawks,
and dives into the sea.
'Wait for us' his friends all call,
and there they are, splashing away.
He comes back with one small fish.
He's got little beads of water on him
and I lead him to his bed.
Flipper, Flipper, Flipper.

Amy Coombs (9)
Norris Bank Primary School

SAVE THE TIGERS

Tiger tiger
silent slider
padding on with velvet paws
often you unsheathe your claws
They shoot you with bullets or drugs
to turn you into tigerskin rugs
Stop it for goodness sake
for soon it will be too late
fur coats and rugs will be their fate.

Elizabeth Ardolino (9)
Norris Bank Primary School

THE DOLPHINS' DAY

Shining, shimmering in the water
so deep, splashing, swishing,
the dolphins eat.
Jumping high, gliding fast,
swimming behind the human's back.

Swimming in schools beneath the rocks,
chasing fish, hiding fast,
before the shark eats up fast,
gobble, gobble, the shark is pleased
because he can feed.

The water's salted,
the moon is shining,
the sea doesn't make a sound.
It is so quiet, the dolphins rest
until it's another restful day.

Claire Bates (9)
Norris Bank Primary School

SPOOKY

S piders all over the place
P lease don't go in this room
      or I will turn you into a frog
O pen the door and look inside
O ut of the door and see a ghost
      in front of you
K eep out of this house
      because it's spooky
Y es, it is spooky in here.

Sophie Cook (5)
Norris Bank Primary School

A Day At School

Every day I go to school,
I don't expect,
Some bloke or fool,
To teach me Maths and English.

Oh look at the time,
Lunch is here,
It's half my rhyme,
Yesss!
It's PE.

It's the end of the week,
It seems so bleak,
That now is the weekend,
But now I dread,
Next week.

Oliver James Robinson (10)
Norris Bank Primary School

Space

Space, doesn't it make you wonder.
How does it start?
How does it end?
In a rocket they sent my best friend
To see if he could find another universe.
But he ended up somewhere worse.
What lives behind planet Mars?
Can it be a lot more stars?
So where does space go?
I guess I'll never know.

Kyle Belt (10)
Norris Bank Primary School

MY LITTLE BROTHER

My little brother is such a pain
He loves splashing in the rain
He loves sweets and ice-cream too
But he never ever eats his stew
His favourite toys are swords and guns
He also likes to make iced buns
He hates bedtimes
He whinges and whines
But he still falls asleep in just one blink
Then you don't hear another wink.

Hannah Louise Firth (11)
Norris Bank Primary School

GORGEOUS CRISPS

The shiny pictures are
glossy. The smell floats up
my nostrils. It is that that
makes me want to keep on eating
crisps.
It is going down like a slide
and it crackles like a bowl of
celery.
It is absolutely fabulous and
salty.
It looks like a small
pancake.
It is curly and you can hear
a crackle.
Then I think this is the best.
When I have eaten them I
want another bag.

Callum Ashton (9)
St Luke's CE Primary School, Warrington

THE WIND

As the wind passes me
I feel a sudden draught.
I feel a thick strong man whistling by.
He blows the autumn leaves around
the forest nature.
The howling wolf is coming today
looking for its prey, waking people
in the night, blowing people's hats.
You see people chasing after them
in an angry temper.
Cartons are flying everywhere.
The wind is just like that.

Daniel Crompton (8)
St Luke's CE Primary School, Warrington

WEEK OF WEATHER

On Monday it was frosty,
no one walked along the road.
On Tuesday it was cloudy and dark,
I did not go to the park.
On Wednesday it was sunny and bright,
I went to fly my kite.
On Thursday it was snowy and white,
I had a very big snowball fight.
On Friday it was rainy and cold,
my head felt it was bald.
On Saturday it was sunny and mild,
I think I might meet a crocodile.
On Sunday I am ready for Monday.

Jon Dutton (7)
St Luke's CE Primary School, Warrington

THE TROUBLE WITH JONATHON

Jonathon was only two,
And thought he was exceedingly thin,
We knew he was getting fatter,
When he invaded the biscuit tin.

Nibble, nibble, munch, munch,
Nibble, nibble, crunch,
He ate the biscuits for lunch.

Jonathon ate a gigantic pizza,
He ate ten thousand bags of chips,
And when he ate an apple,
He swallowed a load of pips.

Nibble, nibble, munch, munch,
Nibble, nibble, crunch,
He ate up all the chips for lunch.

When Jonathon went to McDonald's,
He ate ten thousand egg muffins,
He drank 5 litres of orange,
And then had 60 puffins.

Nibble, nibble, munch, munch,
Nibble, nibble, crunch,
He ate the muffins for lunch.

He ate 10 apples in one go
And he ate a plum,
Then a drum band came along
And then down his throat went a drum.

Nibble, nibble, munch, munch,
Nibble, nibble, crunch,
He ate some apples for lunch.

Jonathon found some false teeth,
Upon the kitchen floor,
He crunched them in his mouth
And spat it out near the door.

Nibble, nibble, munch, munch,
Nibble, nibble, crunch,
He ate false teeth for lunch.

Now surely you can see
How fat Jonathon can be.
He gets in an awful mood
If he doesn't get food!

Nibble, nibble, munch, munch
Nibble, nibble, crunch
Crunch!

Emma James (8)
St Luke's CE Primary School, Warrington

SUPER CRISPS

They are bright and exciting,
They attract me.
My mouth is watering.
My tummy's rumbling.
The smell floats up my
nostrils.
There's a crispy, noisy hard
sound.
Air bubbles float and drift
around.
I feel guilty because I've
finished them all.

Sam Hughes (8)
St Luke's CE Primary School, Warrington

THE GYMNASTIC FLYING SUN

Sun is an angry man, when he wakes up,
he orders everybody to sweat, he makes you
go into your drink section and never come out.
When it goes night-time, the sun suffers from
darkness but the sun never goes away,
it goes to the other side of the solar system.
When it is there it does the same over again.
All its swelling anger drinking in Australia.
The people in Australia have more to drink,
so the sun cannot really strike in Australia.
The sun flies to Canada. He makes it extra hot.
It is like 55°c but he did not get involved.
He flew to Bethlehem. It was hot there too,
so he came and flew back to England.
It meant it was morning so he started his
burning again.

Michael Geeleher (8)
St Luke's CE Primary School, Warrington

THE WIND

Wind can roar like a wolf in the forest.
Wind can be wild and very strong.
Wind can be fierce and blustery.
Wind can be calm and gentle.
Wind is like an angel flying high and low.
Wind can howl.
Wind can be relaxing
and I like relaxing wind, gentle wind and calm wind.
I hate the fierce, blustery, howling and
the wild wind. Oh I do hate strong, wild wind.
It races across my bedroom window,
that gets on my nerves.
Blowing, blustery, fierce, nasty, roaring,
wild wind, I hate that.
Relaxing, gentle, an angel flying high and low
I love that!

Holly Yates (8)
St Luke's CE Primary School, Warrington

THE BIG RED APPLE

Shiny as gold,
Makes me feel hungry,
It's completely round,
Just like a sphere,
Round like a ball,
Smells so juicy and looks delicious
Bite my teeth in
Attacking it, it's sweet
The lovely mush
I lick it
It sticks to my tongue
Juice goes everywhere
The pips brown like seeds
It goes smaller and smaller
The shape goes funny
It's gone cry I go
I swallow it
Down it goes
Down, down
Down into my tum
Yum, yum!

Kerri Dawber (8)
St Luke's CE Primary School, Warrington

THE APPLE EXPERIENCE

There is a red apple sitting in the fruit bowl.
I race my sister to it *yes!* I've got it.
I hold it in the palm of my hand.
Its unusual colour makes it look delicious.
It has dots of white all over it.
I bite into it.
My teeth press on it and I swallow the mush.
I suck juice out of the apple and it trickles down
my long throat.
I bite into it again.
This time I peel off the skin with my teeth and
dig deep into the apple.
Then there is a big white patch in front of me.
I scrape some fruit out of the apple with my
bottom teeth.
Layer upon layer I bite and bite.
My teeth hit something hard.
It's the core!
I nibble round and round the apple
until there is nothing left except the core
and the pips.
That is all about my
apple experience!

Helen Litton (9)
St Luke's CE Primary School, Warrington

CATHERINE PENNINGTON'S AMAZING HAT!

In my amazing hat I will place,
The taste of some chocolate,
Some Popa pants,
A full mouth of the hot boiling sun.

In my amazing hat I will place,
The sound of a kind little puppy,
A ride to the moon,
Two bottles of gold.

In my amazing hat I will place,
The smell of grass,
A jewel from the queen's crown,
A spine-chiller book.

In my amazing hat I will place,
A red rose from Spain,
My dad tidying the house and my mum at the pub,
The sound of the floorboard creaking.

My amazing hat is created out of,
The ashes of fire,
The fresh air we breathe,
The soil of the earth.

I shall hide my hat on an island in Anglesey,
I will only open my hat on my 19th birthday.

Catherine Pennington (9)
St Luke's CE Primary School, Warrington

DINOSAUR TEA

I met a dinosaur once
He had huge scales
And noticeably large gnashers.
He made Arnold Schwarzenegger look like an angel.
His blood-red eyes locked onto their target
Which happened to be me.
'Can I come to tea? I am quite hungry!'
Said he.
I looked at his scales,
I looked at his teeth,
His spines looked like a coral reef!
But all he could say was, 'Can I come to tea? I am very hungry.'
I looked for a place to hide,
I looked for a place that he hadn't spied!
I wanted home,
I wanted peace,
I wanted the police!
I ran and ran with the scaly beast saying, 'Come on let's have a feast!'
I reached my house,
I shut the door,
I fell upon the carpeted floor and said, 'I really want to go to bed,
There is a pounding in my head!'
Just then my dad came home
And broke the dinosaur's every bone.
Then my mum came out and hit it on his lumpy snout!
Sometimes it's nice to have such vicious parents!

Joshua Felton (10)
St Luke's CE Primary School, Warrington

CAROLINE'S TRUNK OF AMAZEMENT

In my trunk I will put,
A slice of cake in a little white bowl,
A big silver spacesuit,
Two whole rainbows and a piece of sun.

And I will put in my trunk,
A swish of an eagle's wing,
A little piece of moon rock,
And three drops of gold.

And I will place in my trunk,
The smell of a beautiful big, pink rose,
A colourful tapestry from Buckingham Palace,
And a star from the sky.

These things will be placed into my trunk,
A poppy from the Caribbean,
A fir tree growing in a hay stack,
And a creak from the stairs.

My trunk is fashioned from,
A spark of fire,
A breath of air,
A piece of stone from the earth,
And a drip of water from Niagara Falls.
I shall keep my trunk at the bottom of a deep blue sea,
guarded by a shark and four dolphins.
I will only open it on the twenty-first of April, in the year
two thousand.

Caroline Fairhurst (9)
St Luke's CE Primary School, Warrington

TIMOTHY'S CHAMPAGNE BOTTLE OF AMAZEMENT!

I will carefully pour into my champagne bottle of amazement,
A tutti-frutti double choc chip nutty ice-cream surprise with all
sauces from all around the world.
A pair of Fila trainers.
100 snow storms so the snow is 100 cm deep.

I will carefully keep in my champagne bottle of amazement,
The terrific roar of a frightening lion.
A two way ticket to Jupiter on an alien's spacecraft
accompanied by aliens themselves.
A crackle of turquoise.

I will carefully store in my champagne bottle of amazement,
The aroma from vegetarian sausages with mustard on top.
A jewel from the queen's crown.
The dark side of the moon on a cold winter's night.

I will carefully collect in my champagne bottle of amazement,
An Arabian cactus from the Atlantic Ocean.
An elephant in a Russian spacecraft.
The sound of my stop watch bleep.

My champagne bottle is created with the cool water of a melted iceberg,
The atmosphere of Jupiter.
A clump of sludge from the River Nile.
A sparkling orange flame.

I will hide my bottle in the great stomach of a humpback whale,
With anemones and lump suckers around it.
I will never open my bottle and its secrets will never be revealed.

Timothy Isherwood (10)
St Luke's CE Primary School, Warrington

THE FAT JUICY APPLE

It's red and shiny,
Hard not soft,
Round and tempting,
Sphere shaped and delicious,
It smells excellent like heaven,
Like the beautiful smell of trees,
I put my teeth against the lovely apple,
And I push against the shiny skin,
Harder, harder,
The juice squirts out,
It tastes lovely,
My teeth munch it,
My tongue twirls it around,
I swallow the crispy apple,
Down, down, down it goes,
Sliping, slurping all the way,
And into my stomach,
I want another bite,
It happens all over again,
Munch, munch, munch,
Down, down, down,
Yum, yum,
It gets smaller and smaller,
And changes shape every bite,
Until there is only the core,
The pips,
And the stork left.
That was great!
Yum, yum!

Katharine Fox (8)
St Luke's CE Primary School, Warrington

SIMPLY THE BEST!

It's got red shiny skin,
It's shaped like a sphere,
It has cold hard skin,
Mmmm . . . it tastes
exquisite and scrumptious,
I crush it and mush it,
My saliva mixes into it,
It's crispy and crunchy
It's really munchy,
My tongue rolls over,
I smile but then it goes to my tum
Yum!
Yum!

Neil Holland (9)
St Luke's CE Primary School, Warrington

SPRING IS IN THE AIR

Spring is in the air
Tulips and daffodils everywhere
Spring lambs dancing in the fields
Smiling faces everywhere
Bluebells carpet the woods around
Blue tits sing amongst the trees
Spring is in the air
Smiling faces everywhere
Mum spring cleans the garden shed
Dad goes and hides his head
Spring is in the air
Smiling faces everywhere.

Vicky Lewis (8)
St Matthew's CE Primary School, Warrington

MY MOM

My mom thinks I'm naughty,
My mom thinks I'm bad,
My mom thinks I'm stupid,
She surely must be mad!

My mom thinks I'm good,
She thinks I drink beer,
My mom thinks I'm great,
Too bad, she's only queer!

My mom thinks I'm ugly,
My mom thinks I'm clever,
My mom thinks I'm a baby,
This sure ain't heaven!

My mom thinks I'm pretty,
She thinks I'm a daisy,
My mom thinks I'm a doll,
Just kidding, she's only *crazy!*

Grace Hatton (8)
St Matthew's CE Primary School, Warrington

FIREWORKS

At first the field is very quiet.
Only the bonfire crackles and pops.
Suddenly the sky sparkles with stars shooting.
Then the Catherine wheel swizzles and swirls spinning round.
Bombs banging and booming,
Bursting through the night sky.
Rockets spreading and shimmering in the sky.
Only a few crackles left in the night.
Then it's over.

Gareth Rowlands (9)
St Matthew's CE Primary School, Warrington

A Day At A Rugby Match

A attacks the wrong player,
B bounces the ball,
C crashes into a post,
D dances on a pitch,
E erased himself,
F flew to score,
G gurgles and falls down,
H hopes to trip over,
I identifies the ball,
J jumps for the ball,
K kicks the commentator,
L lies on the ball,
M mutated into a post,
N navigated to the touch line,
O only came out once,
P pounces on the coach,
Q quarrels with the ref,
R runs and falls,
S slumps to the ground,
T tries to do a dive goal,
U upset the sponsors,
V voted for the wrong team,
W went to weep in the corner,
X explored the pitch,
Y yawned and went off,
Z zipped up and went home.

Stuart McArthur (8)
St Matthew's CE Primary School, Warrington

At A Football Match . . .

A attacks players,
B bounces a ball,
C crosses a ball,
D directs the match,
E exercises on the touchline,
F fouled the players,
G gathers balls,
H heads the balls,
I   ignores the referee,
J jumps to head the ball,
K kicks the ball,
L lives to play football,
M managers mutter,
N knocks the ball,
O outran his opponent,
P practised football,
Q quivered quietly,
R reached up to the ball,
S stretched to save the ball,
T ticked the whole match,
U umpired football,
V vacuumed the football field,
W wished that Liverpool would win,
X x-rayed David Beckham.
Y yawned quietly in the football match,
Z zipped his jacket up on the way
    home from the football match.

Adam Speers (8)
St Matthew's CE Primary School, Warrington

WHY POEM

Why does the world go round?
What is the reason for my life?
Who knows why there's water in the pond?
Why is Stewart's hair blond?
Who knows why?
Why are there so many questions to ask?
Why do we learn to write?
Why do we watch children's TV?
Why, why, why?
Who knows why?
What colour is Saturn?
What, who, why?
Why is no one ten foot tall?
Why are there humans on the earth?
Who knows why?

Peter Morgan (8)
St Matthew's CE Primary School, Warrington

TREES

On a bitter cold winter's night
I was walking though a forest.
It was as misty as a steamed up window.
As I looked up to the sky the tall trees stood
In a row in the moonlight
Like soldiers standing to attention.
As I turned around I was sure that the
Branches of the trees were like arms
Stretched out trying to reach me.
They looked as sharp as a knife
I felt so unwelcomed.

Natalie Gregson (9)
St Matthew's CE Primary School, Warrington

THE SEASHORE

The sea is swishing around my feet.
Clouds like cotton wool floating above my head.
A chilly breeze twisting and turning through my hair.
The cold sea making the hairs on my back stand up.
The only noises I can hear are the wind and the sea.
Everything else is calm, peaceful and still.
A giant cloth of sand tickling my toes.

Jonathan Henshaw (10)
St Matthew's CE Primary School, Warrington

TREES

As I walked through the ghostly, evil trees.
Small and helpless.
And black and brown.
When I walk through the terrifying grass field
with my lost memory.
With the sharp branches poking in my arm.
All lonely and terrifying like a frightened child.

Ashley Platt (9)
St Matthew's CE Primary School, Warrington

WINTER

I was lonely in a field of bare trees
and twisting branches like an octopus.
It was unwelcoming and felt bitter cold.
They looked like they were holding a secret.
I felt small like a matchstick.
The trees pointed like knives.

Natalie Heesom (10)
St Matthew's CE Primary School, Warrington

BONFIRES

B urning wood with crackling flames.
O n the top a Guy Fawkes sits crackling away.
N obody can see you, just hear the pops, bangs and booms.
F izzing sparklers which the children hold.
I n the sky the pops, bangs and booms turn into colours far away.
R ustling paper and wood burning, shrivelling up.
E verlasting, crunching and pops in the orange flames.
S parks crackle away into the dark sky.

Sophie Mills (9)
St Matthew's CE Primary School, Warrington

DARK

It was as black as a witch's black cat's tail,
It was cold outside like ice cubes in a freezer,
It was scary, sad and silent,
It was unlit everywhere,
It was a lazy, lonely, lost like place,
It was uncomfortable unlike my bed,
It was very desolate and weird,
It was winter.

Jenny Hill (11)
St Matthew's CE Primary School, Warrington

HAUNTED HOUSE

There's a haunted house,
On top of a creepy hill,
Who knows what lives there.

Jonathan Nesbitt (9)
St Matthew's CE Primary School, Warrington

A SCARY PLACE

I am in a place with not much colour
which is spooky
and as scary as a haunted house
covered in spider webs
and now and then a ghost jumping out at you.
Spooky and mysterious trees
that seem to hold secrets.
Then after a while if you look
at them closely
they become long and as thin as matchsticks.
They are twisted and as sharp as rope.
Now and then the trees become unwelcoming and crooked.
The place I am standing in has days on end with a plague
which never seems to stop.
But all of a sudden it stops
and it's just a field again
with those weary trees
that seem to give you shivers.

Nicola Wright (9)
St Matthew's CE Primary School, Warrington

LIKE ME WITHOUT YOU

Like bread without butter,
Like rain without gutter,
Like bathrooms without loo,
Like me without you.

Like eyes without sight,
Like ears without sound,
Like mouth without taste,
Like me without you.

Adam Burgess (10)
St Matthew's CE Primary School, Warrington

LIKE ME WITHOUT YOU

Like a tree without twigs,
Like Man U without Giggs,
Like bread that's gone blue,
Like me without you.

Like a bell with no ring,
Like a chess set without a king,
Like a TV you cannot view,
Like me without you.

Like a chair with no legs,
Like a cloakroom with no pegs,
Like a sock without a shoe,
Like me without you.

Like a dog without a tail,
Like Jonah without the whale,
Like a koala with no bamboo,
Like me without you.

Justin Massey (11)
St Matthew's CE Primary School, Warrington

LIKE ME WITHOUT YOU

Like boats without propellers.
Like submarines without torpedoes.
Like animals without a zoo.
Like me without you.

Like a fisherman with no maggots.
Like a Tigger without Winnie the Pooh.
Like a rabbit with no carrots.
Like me without you.

Michael Foat (10)
St Matthew's CE Primary School, Warrington

UNTITLED

I am in a long,
dark,
never ending,
evil lane.
As I slowly walk down this
dark,
never ending lane,
I hear long slow howls from distant beasts.
These howls make me feel so small,
as small
as a small snake.
There are also distant shrieks
from the trees.
But not just any trees,
trees that look like hands,
evil hands
that jump out and grab you
like the hands of a goblin.

Emma Johnson (9)
St Matthew's CE Primary School, Warrington

LIKE ME WITHOUT YOU

Like a church without a vicar
Like a heart without love
Like potatoes without stew
Like me without you.

Like tea without sugar
Like earth without people
Like Norman without Sue
Like me without you.

Robert Cooper (10)
St Matthew's CE Primary School, Warrington

LIKE ME WITHOUT YOU

Like England without Shearer
Like Coronation Street without Vera
Like an arm with no joints
A game with no goal
Like me without you.

Like Superman with no cape
Like a clown without jokes
Like a clock with no time
Like icing with no cake
Like me with no you.

Like butter without the flies
Like under without the wear
Like a T without a shirt
And a grass with no hopper
Like me without you.

Patrick Hughes (10)
St Matthew's CE Primary School, Warrington

SNOW QUEEN

She blows feathers down from the sky,
They land on the ground in blankets of snow.
She makes lace out of silk for snowflakes.
She has hair as white as snow,
Skin as smooth as ice.
Dresses and cloaks finely spun in gossamer silk.
Happiness lasts until winter ends.
Then slowly she melts into a cloud,
And disappears for another year.

Harriet Batey (9)
St Matthew's CE Primary School, Warrington

IN THE FOREST

Trees are spiky as matchsticks,
Twigs that reach out like grabbing hands,
Gloomy, like it holds a secret.
Old,
    Mysterious,
        Almost evil,
Creaky like the whole forest is going to fall on top of me.
Lonely like you are the only person on earth.
You think you are being watched or shadowed,
I turned round, there was nobody there.
        I walked through the crackling trees,
I think the trees are watching me through their invisible eyes,
I walked further and further into the forest,
I felt like an ant next to an elephant.

Jennifer Milner (9)
St Matthew's CE Primary School, Warrington

WINTER

Storms raging like a man
Galloping on his horse.

The skies are dull and plain
And the birds have deserted.

Snowflakes dropping inch by inch
Like the first life of winter.

The wind it rushes through your
Hair and sweeps round every corner.

Elizabeth Evans (8)
St Matthew's CE Primary School, Warrington

THE COLD

The snow is cold
The holly is sharp
And all the cold is outside
But I am inside
By the warm fire
And the cat on my lap
Sitting in front of the TV
I can hear the wind howling
Through the lock
I look through the window
And what do I see?
I see snow, snow falling down from the sky
They look like dancers coming out of the sky
Making a carpet of snow on the ground.

Victoria Semple (8)
St Matthew's CE Primary School, Warrington

DEVIL'S WOOD

I walked through a forest,
it was gloomy as a pitch-black windy night.
The trees were bare, spidery and ghostly,
they looked as if the devil himself had crafted them.
The horizon looked misty and evil,
I heard a strange noise.
The unwelcoming trees were creaking in the wind,
they looked lost, as if they held a secret.
I was terrified, and wondered whether I would
ever get out.

Chris Sutcliffe (9)
St Matthew's CE Primary School, Warrington

WITHOUT YOU

Like bread without butter
Like a sky with no blue
Like a can opener that has no cutter
Like me without you.

Like a window without a shutter
Like a lace with no shoe
Like a golf club that has no putter
Like me without you.

Like a test without a mutter
Like a baby with no coo
Like a house that has no gutter
Like me without you.

Lauren Massey (10)
St Matthew's CE Primary School, Warrington

TREES

Walking through a gloomy place.
Unwelcoming and lonely,
trees as sharp as pins.
Feels like hands coming to get you.
Foggy, vague trees in the distance.
As cold as ice and holds a secret.
Spidery trees feeling haunted,
walking along terrified, horrible,
creepy place.
At last you come to an end.

Stephanie Clements (10)
St Matthew's CE Primary School, Warrington

FEELING BLUE

Like a pizza without cheese
Like a clown without a smile
Like a fan without a breeze
Like me without you.

Like a wood without trees
Like a detective without a clue
Like a flower without bees
Like me without you.

Like a horse without a cart
Like the Air Force with no planes
Like the Simpsons without Bart
Like me with no you.

Stephen Platts (10)
St Matthew's CE Primary School, Warrington

LIKE ME WITHOUT YOU

Like pencils without lead,
Like blankets without beds,
Like colours without blue,
Like me without you.

Like sky with no sun,
No kids out having fun,
Like a fog without mist,
And boxers without fists,
Like pigeons that can't coo
And me without you.

Chris Nesbitt (11)
St Matthew's CE Primary School, Warrington

LIKE ME WITHOUT YOU

Like a house without walls,
Like a horse with flu,
Like a doctor with no calls,
Like me without you.

Like a baby with no mother,
Like colours without blue,
Like a book with no cover,
Like me without you.

Like a pond with no water,
Like a scientist with nothing to do,
Like a father with no daughter,
Like me without *you*.

Emma Perris (10)
St Matthew's CE Primary School, Warrington

SCARED, FRIGHTENED AND LOST

The tree tops are as sharp as pins.
Always bare like at autumn.
The trees are twisted, crooked like an old man.
With spiky branches that have grabbing hands.
I'm scared, frightened and lost.

It's misty and gloomy.
Some trees look like giants up there.
Some are really very small.
I'm scared, frightened and lost.
I really don't like it here at all.

Jonathan Gee (9)
St Matthew's CE Primary School, Warrington

LIKE ME WITHOUT YOU

Like a zebra without stripes,
Like a leopard without spots,
Like a rabbit without fur,
Like me without you.

Like a forest without trees,
Like a whale without blue,
Like the Arctic without its freeze,
Like me without you.

Like a clown without its laugh,
Like a room with no view,
Like a cow with no calf,
Like me without you.

Anna Mathew (10)
St Matthew's CE Primary School, Warrington

TREES

As I am walking,
Along a gloomy field with bare trees,
Spiky and evil.
Sharp pointed trees with no leaves on.
I feel alone,
There's no one there
Except me and the trees.
It's really lonely.
It's like everyone's in a deep sleep.
The trees are so unwelcoming.
It's so cold,
I could turn to ice.

Kirsten Taylor (9)
St Matthew's CE Primary School, Warrington

ME WITHOUT YOU

Like a world without flowers
Like grass without dew
Like someone who never showers
Like me without you.

Like a beach with no sand
Like a sea that's not blue
Like no one to lend a hand
Like me without you.

Like a pond without a reflection
Like a gymnast with no act to do
Like a job seeker with a rejection
Like me without you.

Sally Pitcher (10)
St Matthew's CE Primary School, Warrington

TREES

As I am walking through this gloomy place
wind is blowing down my neck.
Sometimes it feels like someone tapping me on the shoulder.
I turn round, jumping out of my skin.
The trees look like they would jump out at me
any second.
The branches are rattling like old bones.
It is so lonely here.
I feel so small with all the big trees around me.
The place is so unwelcoming.
The atmosphere is so ghostly.
At times I think I see a ghost in the mist.

Elizabeth Hughes (9)
St Matthew's CE Primary School, Warrington

FEELING GLUM WITHOUT YOU

Like an orange without juice.
Like clowns without any jokes.
Like animals without a zoo.
Like me without you.

Like heaven with no god.
Like a wall with no stone.
Like a soldier with no shoe.
Like me without you.

Like a pen with no ink.
Like a kitchen with no sink.
Like a window with no view.
Like me without you.

Matthew Willis (11)
St Matthew's CE Primary School, Warrington

CATS!

Cats are cute
Cats are nice
Cats eat rats
Cats eat mice
worms, frogs, birds, fish,
they *all* end up on the dish
My cat Alfie is ginger and white
if you're not careful he might bite
My cat Cleo is black and white
She is gentle and doesn't bite
Nine lives has each cat
when they are gone that is that.

Georgina Randle (8)
St Matthew's CE Primary School, Warrington

BONFIRE NIGHT

Plop goes the rain into the puddles.
Zoom go the fireworks into the sky.
The bonfire's burning all reds and yellows.
Toffee apples and sticky toffee.
All to be eaten on bonfire night.
The Catherine wheel so bright.
It shimmers in the moonlight.
The fireworks whiz and pop, off they go.
Sparklers shine so when you've lit them,
Move them fast.
They leave a trace of glistening light,
All different colours.
Dazzling.

Harriet Smith (9)
St Matthew's CE Primary School, Warrington

SCARY TREES

I was wandering through the mist when
I saw a monster-like thing.
It was big and had spiky things
sticking out of it.
It looked scary like a witch trying
to cast a spell.
Then I walked a bit closer, it
looked a bit like a tree.
It was a normal tree,
it was still quite scary and it
did look like a monster.
So I decided to run.
I ran until I got home.

Mark Allen (9)
St Matthew's CE Primary School, Warrington

Mr White's Fright!

Mr White was in a fright
on a spooky Friday night
He saw a ghost flying round
a lamppost.

He ran a mile through the woods
but there was a ghost eating spuds
He looked in front, he looked behind
His pants fells down and he started to cry.

He went back home very embarrassed
His face was red he wondered why
His wife came in and gave a loud cry
and then she gave a very long sigh.

He went to bed and banged
his head
He woke up in the morning
and his face was red.

Eleanor Elliott (11)
St Paul of the Cross RC Primary School, Warrington

Apples Are Good For You

It looks very small like a rubber ball.
It looks rough like a stone.
It looks shiny like the sun.
It feels rough and hard like the wall.
It smells like apple juice.
It feels very hard.
It tastes like 100 apples in my throat.

Kimberley Jane Rimmer (8)
St Paul of the Cross RC Primary School, Warrington

FOOD

Party cake
Wobbly jelly
Eat a lot and
Fill your belly.

Fatty bacon
Tasty chips
Blazing burgers and
Winter nips.

Crunchy chicken
Hot hot dogs
Yellow cheese and
Christmas logs.

Lovely chocolate
Watery pears
Tangy sherbet and
Teddy bears.

Pumpkin pie
Thin ham
Fresh green lettuce and
Chewy lamb.

Orange carrots
Smelly fish
There's all this food
So pile your dish!

Beth Conroy (10)
St Paul of the Cross RC Primary School, Warrington

SPACE

Space is danger
Flashing bright
Don't go there
you'll get a fright
With green wobbling
aliens, footballs for
their eyes
laughing hyenas
no that's not right.

I saw a crater
in the middle was a baker
It was dusty
and musty
It made me cough
the ground was rough
and very tough

I'm glad it was
a dream
but is was quite
supreme.

Zowie Slevin (11)
St Paul of the Cross RC Primary School, Warrington

SHIMMERING, GLOOMY SHADOWS AT NIGHT

I feel I'm trapped
in a bear's gloomy cave
but instead of the bear
in the cave there are shadows
that make me terrified
a car comes
it splashes light over my room
my room glows like winter snow
now I think I'm not alone
now there's no lock
there's no escape
I'm surrounded by beastly demon shadows
my heart is beating fast
I stretch the cover over me
arrrrr, help, I pulled the cover over my eyes
I'm shaking in the velvet darkness.

David Capper (9)
St Paul of the Cross RC Primary School, Warrington

I WANT TO BE AN ASTRONAUT

I want to be an astronaut flying into space,
bang off I go, zooming for a race.

I want to be an astronaut flying like a bird,
I want to be like Paul Jones who broke the world record.

I want to be an astronaut looking down at land,
everyone will see me as I wave my hand.

Joanna Brzezicki (7)
St Paul of the Cross RC Primary School, Warrington

SWEET SONG

This is the sweet song
Song of the sweets
Liquorice and sherbet
And lots of yummy treats

Butterscotch and chocolate
Cola bottles too
Multi-coloured Smarties
And little toffee chews

Pink rock and candy bears
Peppermints, fruit treats
Pear drops and raspberry drops
For everyone to eat!

Misa Brzezicki (10)
St Paul of the Cross RC Primary School, Warrington

WHAT IS THE MOON?

The moon is a Catherine wheel
without the colour.
The moon is a round piece
of smelly cheese without the taste.
The moon is a round tea bag
without the brown tea.
The moon is a nought without the hole.
The moon is a clock without the black numbers.
The moon gives us light by night.

Anna Burgess (8)
St Paul of the Cross RC Primary School, Warrington

MAGIC SNEAKERS

I have a pair of magic sneakers
that bounce me into space
I fly up to Saturn
and on its rings I race.

I have a pair of magic sneakers
and they pounce me to Mars
I watch all the comets go by
and photograph the shooting stars.

I have a pair of magic sneakers
they shoot me to the moon
I went into an alien school
and their heads looked like balloons.

James Procter (8)
St Paul of the Cross RC Primary School, Warrington

MYSTERY CREATURES

They eat lamb and meat
and some have smelly feet.
Some of them have collections
and they enjoy Cadbury's selections.
Lots of them like maths and
some even go to the swimming baths.
Some dance, some prance, once at
school they play planet chance.
These are you people, you might
well ask have you figured out
the task?

Jemma Brindle (9)
St Paul of the Cross RC Primary School, Warrington

MAGIC FLIP FLOPS

I have a pair of magic flip flops
that flip flop me up to the stars
and if they have enough energy
they'll take me up to Mars

I have a pair of magic flip flops
that take me up to space
I see some little aliens
that want to have a race

I have a pair of magic flip flops
that help me win the race
one even catches a blob of mud
and splats an alien in the face.

Jamie Newton (8)
St Paul of the Cross RC Primary School, Warrington

FRIENDS

As friends we gossip, babble, call,
in the playground by the wall.

As friends we stroll, shuffle, plod,
in the garden we will nod.

As friends we are merry, cheerful, glad,
we are never sad.

As friends we help, lend a hand,
then we play in the playground.

As friends we love, care and be good,
we will give a little nudge.

Teresa Cunningham (9)
St Paul of the Cross RC Primary School, Warrington

TEN SNOWMEN

10 cold snowmen standing in a line
1 fell over then there were 9.

9 dumb snowmen in a test
1 was great then there were 8.

8 dead snowmen in a funeral
1 went to heaven then there were 7.

7 silly snowmen playing with sticks
1 dropped one then there were 6.

6 stupid snowmen playing with a hive
1 got stung then there were 5.

5 tall snowmen walking through a door
1 banged its head then there were 4.

4 slippy snowmen climbing a tree
1 fell out then there were 3.

3 happy snowmen playing a game
1 didn't know what to do then there were 2.

2 hungry snowmen going to the shops
All the food was gone then there was 1.

1 sporty snowman racing itself
Whoosh! It was gone, then there were none.

Laura Slater (10)
St Simon's RC Primary School, Stockport

FAT CAT

Fat cat on the wall
Sitting up straight and tall
On the wall all day
Until the sun fades away.

The cat slowly goes to sleep
And not another single peep
Dreaming all through the night
Until the sun shines very bright.

Lucy Hook (10)
St Simon's RC Primary School, Stockport

MAGIC!

I awoke one morning to find
my toes frozen and my lips blue.
This could only mean one thing - snow.
I tore back the curtains
and flung open the window
to reveal a white heaven . . . magic!
I must have stood for quite some time,
looking at the tiny pawprints
and the robin searching for food.
I couldn't pull my eyes away
from the glistening new world . . . magic!
I fled down the stairs to take a better look.
Then it hit me, to get dressed.
I fled down the stairs once more,
flung open the door
and stepped out . . . magic!
The soft sound of my feet
sinking into the snow,
got louder and louder as I started to run.
My heart pounded,
then I stopped and realised
I had disturbed the . . . magic!

Victoria Turner (11)
St Simon's RC Primary School, Stockport

THE TEN SNOWMEN

10 freezing snowmen shivering in a row,
1   tumbled over, now there are 9.
9   happy snowmen having a barbecue,
1   quickly melted, now there are 8.
8   sporty snowmen having a football match,
1   got sent off, now there are 7.
7   clever snowmen having a maths exam,
1   got sent out now there are 6.
6   sad snowmen standing in a row,
1   got blown away, now there are 5,
5   childish snowmen climbing up a tree,
1   got slit in half, now there are 4.
4   warm snowmen standing in a row,
1   got too hot, now there are 3.
3   animal snowmen standing in a farm,
1   stood in horse much, now there are 2.
2   kind snowmen giving each other presents,
1   danced with glee, now there is 1.
1   unhappy snowman smoking on a pipe,
       He died of cancer, now there are none.

Simon Nicholls (10)
St Simon's RC Primary School, Stockport

WINTER

W inter is cold, icy and windy.
I   ce is slippery and cold.
N othing is as cold as winter.
T wirling winds blowing everything away.
E njoy playing in the snow.
R ain and snow fall from the sky.

Ella Newton (10)
St Simon's RC Primary School, Stockport

CAT'S WINTER

I looked out of my window,
and took a great big gasp.
Upon my window ledge,
were millions of icicles wedged.
I crept down the wooden stairs,
where my cat met me with a scare.
'You silly cat, don't ever do that.
I'll let you out I promise I will,
Just let me get down the stairs.'
I opened the door very quickly,
and saw a blanket of snow.
The cat shot out like a bullet.
Like a bullet out of a gun.
And all I could see in the blanket of snow
were little, tiny
            pawprints!

Annie May Meek (11)
St Simon's RC Primary School, Stockport

WINTER

W inter winds are freezing cold.
I ce-skating is good fun.
N early Christmas Eve.
T ime to eat Christmas pudding.
E very day we go to play in the snow.
R eindeer getting ready to fly.

Christopher Simpson (10)
St Simon's RC Primary School, Stockport

My House In Winter

The first thing anyone would have noticed,
was the ground covered in ice-cream.
Next were the frozen, clear, icicles
hanging from the drainpipe above.
The snow like a white feather
floating from heaven to earth.
Frost patterns on the window,
I knew that Jack Frost had visited that night!
A big gust of wind blew the snow from our bin,
and danced in the air like a turning blizzard.
Brittle roses, their stems and petals dying slowly,
slowly to the ground.
I hope the snow, the snow in the picture frame,
will stay, just one more day.

Ruth Monaghan (10)
St Simon's RC Primary School, Stockport

Blizzard

B lustery winds
L ightly landing on the ground
I cicles sticking out of roofs
Z ooming around the country
Z ooming faster and faster
A nasty blizzard is in the air
R oofs are flying in the air, that is a scare
D rifting winds.

Michael Guest (10)
St Simon's RC Primary School, Stockport

Snow!

I'm sat near the fire
Looking outside
Talking to the snow.
'How do you fall
From the sky so gently?
How do you cover
The streets with your fluffy snow?'
Looking as white as a sheet
I like to go playing
In the snow I tell it
I'm glad we have snow.

Lara Dickson (10)
St Simon's RC Primary School, Stockport

Snowdrop

Snow is as cold as the night air,
Snow is as white as a cloud,
Snow is as quiet as a mouse,
Snow drifts like a bird,
Snow is as crunchy as autumn leaves,
Snow is like silvery flakes,
Snow is like woolly petals,
Snow is like a blizzard.

Sarah Louise Kelly (10)
St Simon's RC Primary School, Stockport

SNOW

Snow, snow, why are you white?
Snow, snow, you give me delight.
Snow, snow, why are you light?
Snow.
Snow, snow, why do you fall?
Snow, snow, on the wall.
Snow.
Snow, snow, as light as a feather.
Snow, snow, some bunched together.
Snow, snow, always forever.
Snow.

Samantha Wilson (10)
St Simon's RC Primary School, Stockport

WE'RE BEST FRIENDS

You're my friend, I'm your friend
We're best friends
We laugh, we play, we joke
We're best friends
We tell each other our secrets
We're best friends
No one can split us up because
We're best friends forever!

Laura Gavin (10)
St Simon's RC Primary School, Stockport

FROSTY MORNINGS

The window is full of frosty
Patterns,
Like a carving in ice,
It bites the glass like a mouse,
But beyond the frosty window,
What a beautiful sight to see,
Everywhere covered in white,
It's like a sheet covering
this delightful tree with ice,
On this beautiful frosty morning.

Rachel Ann Iaconianni (10)
St Simon's RC Primary School, Stockport

PICK A NUMBER!

Pick a number! Pick a number!
Think hard and concentrate.
Could it be six, fifteen or eight?
Each number you pick decides our fate.
An anniversary, birthday or a number on our gate.
Hurry and choose them, we dare not be late.
Why are we rushing?
What could it be . . . ?
The Saturday night lottery!

Natalie Brunker (11)
St Simon's RC Primary School, Stockport

SNOWFLAKE

S nowflakes drifting like feathers
N asty blizzards in the air
O n a cold day
W histling wind is scary
F ires are nice and warm
L ightly landing on the ground
A nasty wind in the air
K nock on the door because you are cold
E nough coldness for a day, let's get warm.

James Harrison (11)
St Simon's RC Primary School, Stockport

SPACE

If I went into space
I'd sit on the moon.
If I went into space
I'd find other life forms.
If I went into space
I'd go to the red planet Mars.
If I went into space
I'd fly across the stars.
If I went into space
I'd fly through the galaxy.
If I went into space
I'd see if the moon was
Really made of cheese.
If I went into space
And I saw an alien
I'd fly away and scream.

Sarah-Jane Davies (10)
Woolston CE Primary School

SPACE

Mars, the planet of war
dangerous and mean
silent and quick
Mars, the red planet

Mercury, the messenger
sad and depressing
catches everything with a glimpse
Mercury, the nosy planet

Venus, the planet of peace
calm and motionless
peaceful and tranquil
Venus, the quiet planet

Pluto, so far away
so cold and gloomy
so icy and still
Pluto, the freezing, killing planet

Saturn, a ring on a finger
the immense, large planet
most recognised, but weary
Saturn, my favourite planet

Uranus, a Saturn 'wannabe'
a small, yet beautiful place
though disappointing in size
Uranus, is a private, plump planet.

Craig Mannion (10)
Woolston CE Primary School

MY SPACE JOURNEY

This suit feels very baggy
I feel like a balloon.
The front panel (which you look through)
is very clean.
I stepped into the spaceship,
it was massive!
I couldn't believe what I was seeing,
but it was complicated
there were a hundred buttons,
joysticks and brakes
although the one which caught my eye
was the launch button.
That was the one which was
going to fire me into space.
10,9,8,7 . . .
I felt nervous and tense
my heart pounded.
My seat-belt was tight.
Whoosh we were off.
The space craft jolted
and crashed into space.
There was a deafening rumbling sound
as we blasted into space.
Suddenly everything changed
I felt weightless and calm.
Everything was still.
It was dark, empty and felt never ending.
We came to a crashing halt.
I stepped out.
Wow! We had landed on the moon.
The ground was rock-solid and crusty.
I felt happy that we had arrived.

It was like a lost world.
As we walked we left dusty footprints.
All too soon it was time to go back.
It felt brilliant that I had been on the moon.

Vinu Giridharan (10)
Woolston CE Primary School

THE SPACE JOURNEY

5 . . . 4 . . . 3 . . . 2 . . . 1 . . . *lift off!*
Sat in a spaceship, shaking all around.
I looked out of the window all I see is land.
An hour later I look out of the window,
all that I see there is a round ball.
Bang! I've stopped, the ship's door immediately opens.
I steadily climb out of the ship, I'm now a floaty person
in a spacesuit,
I start to float around on top of the cheesy moon.
I steady myself and land back on the moon.
Bee-p! Its horn has sounded
I have to be quick or the ship's door will close.
I float slowly and steadily back to the ship.
The door closes with a massive *bang!*
'Here we go,' I said. The ship started with a zoom.
I'm off, I start to shake. We're still moving very fast.
We're slowing down, steadily,
As I get out of the spacesuit everyone asks
'How did it go?'
and I said, 'It was an excellent journey.'

Claire Louise Delooze (10)
Woolston CE Primary School

SPACE TRAVEL

We have lift off!
I was off, to seek new planets and stars,
to find life on other planets
never seen before.
Our space shuttle suddenly burst
through the earth's atmosphere
I was travelling at such speeds
I felt suicidal.
After the mask of bravery
I looked outside the shuttle,
I saw all the stars in their dazzling night
colours all scattered around the solar system.
Stars in their thousands.
The galaxy lay still and motionless.
Behold a great planet of ice
I zoomed past it within seconds!
When suddenly I came across a huge black hole!
I then decided to turn back
I went into top drive and headed away
from the great mysteries of space.

Ricky Postlethwaite (10)
Woolston CE Primary School

SPACE

Walk upon the silver sand
plunge across the grey moon land
See the stars in the sky
grab a moonbeam as I pass by
See the earth so round and still, so blue
and beautiful, like a dream come true.

Luanne Jones (11)
Woolston CE Primary School

124

AROUND THE WORLD IN EIGHTY DAYS

England, Africa, America, France
All look different from way up here.
Counting countries counting stars
All very difficult from way up here.
Passing days illuminated with stars
All so funny from way up here.
Icy air never moving with the breeze
All so queer from way up here.
Visible landmarks of human habitation
Not so great from way up here.
Everything's great with stunning views
All so lonely way up here!

Lisa Yates (11)
Woolston CE Primary School

SPACE

Spacesuits are very uncomfortable.
I felt confused and very scared
I was squashed and relaxed
And nearly falling asleep.
I looked out of the window
And I saw Mars.
Cool Mars!
It was so quiet on the moon
And very hard and dusty
Grey and dusty
But I had arrived.

Simon Lee Skelton (10)
Woolston CE Primary School

IF I WAS AN ALIEN

If I was an alien, I'd just sit there on the moon
staring into space.
If I was an alien, I'd scare the life out of all
the spacemen.
If I was an alien, I'd fly my spaceship all
day long.
If I was an alien, I'd take a fast ride on a
speeding comet.
If I was an alien, I'd have green scales
all over me.
If I was an alien, I'd have three eyes
and legs.
If I was an alien, I'd have four arms.
If I was an alien, I'd visit the red
planet Mars.
If I was an alien, I'd visit the Milky Way.
If I was an alien, I'd look down on
Earth and smile.

Daniel Cragg (10)
Woolston CE Primary School

SPACE JOURNEY

When I walked into the shuttle it was very
substantial and complicated.
It felt very delicate and I knew it would be dangerous.
Just before take off I heard a loud noise
it sounded like a disaster.

Zooming through the earth's atmosphere
felt like we were going to plummet back downwards again.
When I looked out of the window, earth was clearly illuminated.

When I saw the moon it was very gloomy and made
me feel depressed. I descended the steps of an Eagle
and I stepped onto the moon.
It was the best day of my life. I was very proud.

Liam Birchall (11)
Woolston CE Primary School

THE PLANETS

When I was three I asked my mummy,
'On Mars do they grow Mars bars,
do they Mummy, do they?'

When I was four I asked my mummy,
'In the Milky Way do they make
Milky Bars, do they Mummy, do they?'

When I was five I asked my mummy,
'Is the moon a big banana, is it Mummy, is it?'

When I was six I asked my mummy,
'Are the galaxies made out of Galaxy bars,
are they Mummy, are they?'

When I was seven I asked my mummy,
'Why did I ask those stupid questions when
I was younger, why Mummy, why?'

Everything is made out of jelly and custard,
of course!

Hannah Harris (11)
Woolston CE Primary School

KNOWING . . .

Of all the mysteries ever been
Of all the stars and planets seen
Of all the journeys taken in space
Has anyone yet seen an alien's face
Apart from the faces we already know
Is there life out there?
I don't know.

Somewhere out there
In that vast lonely space
There must be other beings
There must be another face
Out there in the universe
We cannot be alone
But it will probably take a miracle
For it ever to be known.
Apart from the faces we already know
Is there life out there?
I hope so.

Kirstie Slingsby (11)
Woolston CE Primary School

SPACE THE INFINITE PLACE

This is the peaceful, tranquil space,
This is the place,
The peculiar place in space,
This is space,
The infinite place.

This is the moon out in space,
These are stars,
The extravagant stars,
This is Mars,
The wonderful red, red planet,
This is space,
The infinite place.

Daniel Shaw (11)
Woolston CE Primary School

SPACE

Drifting into space,
I never knew how illuminated it is
with beautiful sparkling stars.
Motionless, peaceful and enchanted.
How tranquil it is.

I can see earth! The wonderful planet itself.
It's extraordinary just being on it, but seeing it from
a bird's eye view!
Magnificent!

Well, now I can see the sun, setting over the earth,
I wish I could come here every day!
An excellent experience it was.
Drifting back from space.

Amie Dolan (10)
Woolston CE Primary School

A DREAM COME TRUE

When I was young, I used to dream,
Of being an astronaut and going to space.
I never thought I'd get there though,
But I didn't really care.
I used to have a telescope,
And look into the stars,
Thousands and thousands of twinkling lights,
Like thousands of fireflies dancing in the night sky.

But now I'm here, in outer space,
It's like a dream come true.
That one step closer to the stars and the planets,
But they're still a million miles away though.

Alex Douglas (10)
Woolston CE Primary School

MY SPACE JOURNEY

Fly me into space
Take me to the place
Where the stars are shining in your eyes
Where the planets are glowing in the dark sky
With the stars
The stars and planets are nice together

In the darkness with the moon
You land me back to earth all too soon.

Craig Fitzsimons (11)
Woolston CE Primary School

I AM THE CHOSEN ONE

I am the chosen one
I must go up
To see the stars and moon above

I am the chosen one
Putting my spacesuit on
Cold and stiff I plod around like an
Angry monster

I am the chosen one
Unsure and alone
Nervous of the journey
I want to go home

I am the chosen one
And I am off
My head thrown back with the
Speed of a rocket

I am the chosen one
The ship's landed
I float out of the door
Onto the dust covered planet
Leaving my prints behind

I am the chosen one
It's time to go home
I hop in the rocket
All on my own

I was the chosen one
I have been up
To see the stars and moon above.

Anna Jones (10)
Woolston CE Primary School

ANOTHER WORLD

The minute I was crammed into my spacesuit,
And strapped into my seat tightly,
I thought about the journey ahead of me,
I considered turning back,
But it was too late,
My ship was already hurtling through space.

I took my seat-belt off,
I started drifting around the craft,
Grabbed hold of the window,
The amazing view filled my eyes,
With the overwhelming view of the Earth!

Swirls of clouds carefully wrapped around it,
It looked very peaceful,
I couldn't imagine that people,
Tiny people, lived there,
I glanced in the opposite direction,
Wow! The moon!

I stepped onto the dusty surface,
It was dented with craters,
I started walking,
I felt light and motionless,
Balancing,
Taking my time,
This is marvellous!

Suddenly I heard a voice on my radio,
'Get in the ship, come home!'
I stumbled into the craft,
And started to go home,
What a *magical* journey,

On another world!

Collette Barker (11)
Woolston CE Primary School